Editor
Mara Ellen Guckian

Editor in Chief
Brent L. Fox, M. Ed.

Creative Director
Sarah M. Fournier

Cover Artist
Sarah Kim

Illustrator
Mark Mason

Art Coordinator
Renée Mc Elwee

Imaging
Amanda R. Harter
Crystal-Dawn Keitz

Publisher
Mary D. Smith, M.S. Ed.

For standards correlations, please visit *http://www.teachercreated.com/standards/*.

Author
Lenore Foster

Teacher Created Resources
12621 Western Avenue
Garden Grove, CA 92841
www.teachercreated.com

ISBN: 978-1-4206-8264-9

Reprinted, 2023
Made in U.S.A.

Teacher Created Resources

Table of Contents

Table of Contents *(cont.)*

Earth and Space Science

Introduction

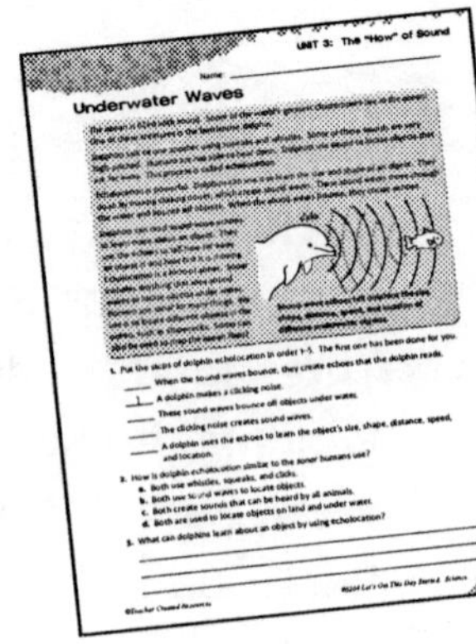
Underwater Waves

Science is the study of the world around us. Students experience science every day without knowing it! Learning about how the world works can be fascinating, but sometimes, students are intimidated or confused by complex science concepts. This book seeks to break down big ideas, such as energy, weathering, and plate tectonics, making them more accessible for fourth-grade students. The passages in this book contain high-interest topics that are aligned with NGSS standards for the grade level. From exploring how roller coasters harness energy to discovering strange animals and their adaptations, students will enjoy practicing their informational reading skills with interesting science topics.

Survival in the Desert

This book is arranged into three sections:

Physical Science

Life Science

Earth and Space Science

Within each section are a number of units, each of which explores an important science topic. Each unit has 4 to 6 pages. Many pages feature reading passages and response questions. Some pages include science-related worksheets. Within each science discipline, the units are sequential and build upon one another. Pages are sequential within a unit, so it is best to work through each section in order.

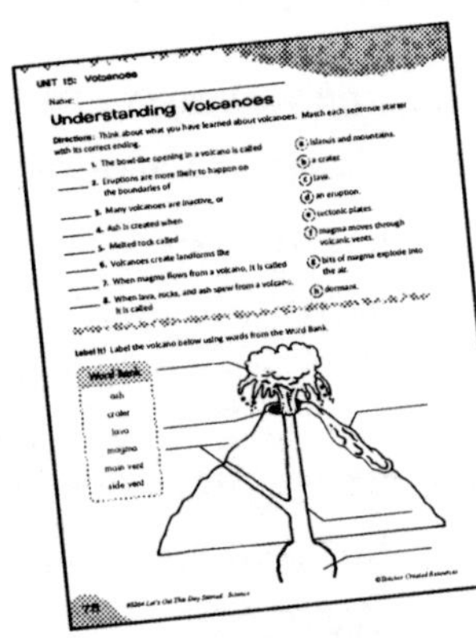
Understanding Volcanoes

Some units incorporate photographs in student activities. These add a realistic element to the writing prompts and engage students by providing real-life connections for their learning. When making photocopies of these pages, it is best to use the photo setting so the images are easier to see. You may also choose to supplement certain passages with related photographs or other visual aids you might have available.

Teachers should not feel restricted by a daily warm-up activity. Sometimes, schedules change. A morning assembly, a make-up lesson, or just an extra-busy day can easily throw off the classroom schedule for days. A teacher never knows what his or her week is going to look like. *Let's Get This Day Started: Science* units do not need to be completed every day or even every other day. Teachers can take their time and arrange the activities to fit their own schedules. A teacher may choose to do a unit a week or spread a unit out over a few weeks. There is no right or wrong way.

These pages are meant to supplement, not substitute for, a science curriculum. Use them in conjunction with science lessons whenever possible.

How to Use This Book

When introducing each new science topic, a teacher may choose to have the class read the passages together as a group before asking them to read each passage again on their own. A teacher may also choose to have students reread passages after a science lesson or unit to reinforce and review learning.

Another way to introduce a new science topic is to begin with the Word Study activity sheet included in each unit. A teacher may choose to review the science vocabulary as a group before reading the passages. This will encourage students to become acquainted with some of the more difficult terms and be on the lookout for them in the passages they will read.

The multiple-choice questions in *Let's Get This Day Started: Science* assess all levels of comprehension—from recall to critical thinking. These questions offer an opportunity to teach students test-taking skills. If an answer choice includes an unfamiliar word, the correct answer can still be found using the process of elimination. Remind students to read every answer choice. If the answer doesn't jump out at them, they can get it right by crossing out the wrong answers first.

The missing words or phrases for fill-in-the-blank questions can be found within the reading passage. These questions reinforce important scientific vocabulary and concepts.

Short, written-response questions require students to connect new learning and vocabulary to their own experiences or to apply the concepts in the passage to new situations. These questions are intended to encourage students to "show what they know," and responses will vary based on your students' reading, writing, and thinking development.

Use the *Tracking Sheet* on page 107 to keep track of which passages you have given to your students, or distribute copies of the sheet for students to monitor their own progress.

An answer key is provided in the back, beginning on page 108. It is important to review how students have answered written-response questions. These answers will vary depending on a student's experiences and prior knowledge.

Tracking Sheet

Unit 1 *(pages 6–10)*
Defining Energy
Hold on Tight!
Potential or Kinetic Energy
Energy Forms
Word Study—Intro to Energy
I See Energy
Unit 2 *(pages 11–15)*
Let There Be Light!
Light Waves
Word Study—The Power of Light
Understanding Light Waves
My Science Blog—Light Energy
Unit 3 *(pages 16–22)*
All About Sound
Light and Sound
Underwater Waves
Dolphin Echolocation
Word Study—The How of Sound
A Dolphin Tale
Unit 4 *(pages 23–27)*
Changes in Energy
Energy Conversions
Word Study—Energy: Conversions and Collisions
Crash! Boom! Pow!
Energy at Work: Baseball
Unit 5 *(pages 28–32)*
Natural Wonder
Waves Are Natural Wonders
Deadly Waves
Word Study—The Wonder of Waves
Writing the Waves
Unit 6 *(pages 33–37)*
Eye Spy
In the Eye
Seeing in the Dark
Word Study—Light and Sight
Is Light Important?

Unit 7 *(pages 38–42)*
The Wonders of the Human Brain
The Three Parts of the Brain
A Day in the Great Outdoors
Word Study—The Human Brain
The Power of the Brain
Unit 8 *(pages 43–47)*
Fennec Foxes—Tiny but Tough
Survival in the Desert
The Sneaky Sidewinder
Word Study—Surviving in the Wild
Adapting to the Desert
Unit 9 *(pages 48–51)*
Groups in the Wild
Understanding Animal Groups
Word Study—Animal Groups
Protecting the Young
Writing About Animal Groups
Unit 10 *(pages 52–56)*
Growing Together
Photosynthesis
Anatomy of a Plant
Word Study—What a Plant Needs to Grow
The Structure of a Plant
Unit 11 *(pages 57–61)*
Let's Rock and Roll!
Three Kinds of Rocks
Reading the Rocks
Word Study—Rock Types
Rock Comics
Unit 12 *(pages 62–66)*
Forces of Nature
Three Types of Weathering
Carried Away
Word Study—Weathering and Erosion
Weathering vs. Erosion
Unit 13 *(pages 67–70)*
Blast from the Past
A Fantastic Find
Word Study—Fossils
Featuring Fossils

Unit 14 *(pages 71–74)*
Journey Through Earth
Earth's Layers
Word Study—Layers of Earth
My Great Journey
Unit 15 *(pages 75–79)*
Kaboom!
Word Study—Volcanoes
Parts of a Volcano
Understanding Volcanoes
On Krakatoa
Unit 16 *(pages 80–83)*
Terrible Temblors
Word Study—Earthquakes
Three Types of Plate Boundaries
Writing About Earthquakes
Unit 17 *(pages 84–89)*
Ready for Anything
Superior Structures
Word Study—Preparing for Earthquakes
The Taipei 101 Skyscraper
Thinking Like an Engineer
Unit 18 *(pages 90–95)*
Flood Alert!
Word Study—Floods
A Safer Space
Preparing for a Flood
Flood Ready
Unit 19 *(pages 96–100)*
Earth's Resources
Types of Resources
The Fuel of Modern Life
Word Study—Natural Resources
My Science Blog—Natural Resources
Unit 20 *(pages 101–106)*
The Way We Live Matters
Types of Pollution and How to Help
Start a Movement!
Word Study—Reducing Our Impact
Pollution I See
My Movement

©Teacher Created Resources #8264 Let's Get This Day Started: Science 107

Name: ______________________________

Defining Energy

Energy makes things happen. It allows us to run, jump, and play. It powers cars, boats, and planes. Energy makes plants and flowers grow. It allows us to think, breathe, and live.

Energy has many forms. It is found in heat, light, and sound. That's just to name a few! Energy can change from one form to another. Think about how solar panels work. They change the Sun's energy into electricity. Energy also changes forms when you are on the move. If you run across a field, the chemical energy in your body changes into moving energy. There are many ways in which energy changes forms.

Though energy can change forms, the total amount of energy in the world *never* changes. This **amount**, or quantity, always stays the same. New energy cannot be created. It also cannot be destroyed. The energy you use to throw a ball or pump a flat tire has been around since the start of the universe!

1. Which of the following defines *energy*?
   - **a.** a type or kind of something
   - **b.** the ability of something to be active or do work
   - **c.** to become larger, to increase in size
   - **d.** a form of energy that is used to operate machines
2. Which of the following about energy is *not* true?
   - **a.** Energy has many different forms.
   - **b.** Energy allows us to work, play, and grow.
   - **c.** Energy can only power small objects.
   - **d.** The Sun's energy can be used to create electricity.
3. Which of the following is true about the *amount* of energy in the universe?
   - **a.** Energy can be destroyed but not created.
   - **b.** The amount of energy in the universe has always stayed the same.
   - **c.** The amount of energy in the universe decreases a little each year.
   - **d.** Energy can be created but not destroyed.
4. Use complete sentences to describe an example of energy in your daily life.

____

____

____

Name: ______________________________

Hold on Tight!

It was Jane's birthday, and she was spending the day at an amusement park. Jane *loved* roller coasters. Her favorite rides were full of twists, turns, and drops.

Jane was excited. There was a new coaster at the park! Before her visit, Jane had spent a lot of time learning about the new ride. During her research, she had learned that coasters are powered by different types of energy.

One type is called **potential energy**. This is stored energy. It is not being used. When a train is stopped at the top of a coaster's drop, it has a lot of potential energy. This is because of the train's position. The farther the train is from the ground, the more potential energy it has. When the train zooms down the coaster, it has **kinetic energy.** This is the type of energy an object has when it is in motion.

Soon, it was Jane's turn to ride the coaster. She raised her arms during its turns and twists. As the train sped along the track, Jane knew kinetic energy was at work. Once the ride was over, the train stopped. When it came to coasters, Jane preferred kinetic energy to potential energy!

1. Which of the following correctly describes *potential energy*?
   - **a.** moving energy that depends on speed
   - **b.** stored energy that is determined by position
   - **c.** roller coaster energy that is designed by architects
   - **d.** light-related energy that depends on heat

2. What does the word *kinetic* likely mean?
   - **a.** staying in one place or position
   - **b.** to cause something new to happen
   - **c.** relating to the movement of physical objects
   - **d.** an idea that someone suddenly thinks of

3. Describe the difference between *kinetic energy* and *potential energy*.

____

____

____

____

Name: ______________________________

Potential or Kinetic Energy?

Directions: Study the image below. Then, decide whether the following phrases are examples of potential or kinetic energy. Write **P** for *potential* or **K** for *kinetic* on each line.

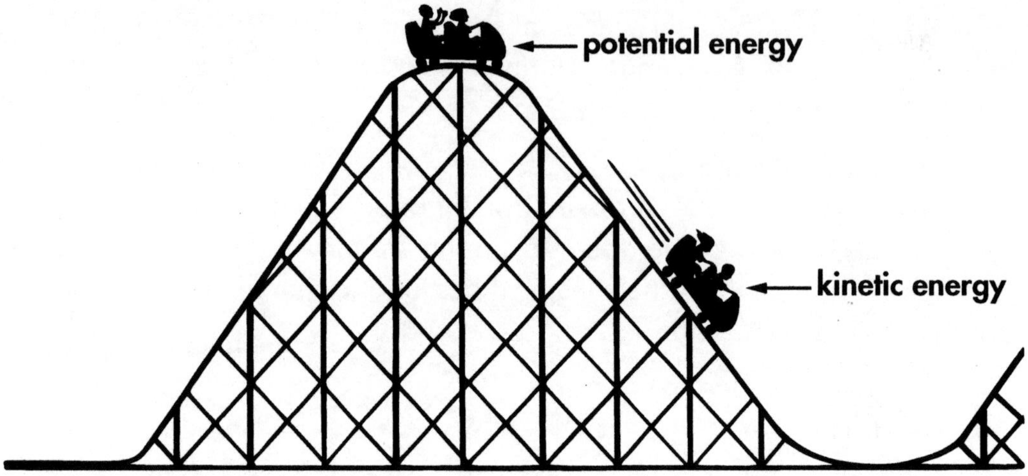

1. __________ rocket launching into space
2. __________ person tying a shoe
3. __________ sitting in a stopped car
4. __________ passing a basketball
5. __________ waiting on a surfboard for a wave
6. __________ pitcher holding a baseball
7. __________ running through the park
8. __________ a bird sitting on a branch
9. __________ swimming in the ocean
10. __________ a person about to ski down a mountain

Draw It! Draw one example of *potential energy* and one example of *kinetic energy* in the box.

Name: ______________________________

Energy Forms

Directions: Think about what you have learned about energy. Match each sentence starter with its correct ending.

_______ **1.** The total amount of energy

_______ **2.** Moving energy is called

_______ **3.** Stored energy is called

(a) kinetic energy.

(b) potential energy.

(c) cannot be created or destroyed.

Word Study—Intro to Energy

Directions: Study the words and definitions. Then, use each vocabulary word in a sentence that relates to the information from this unit.

energy—the ability of something to be active or do work

____

____

kinetic energy—energy relating to the movement of physical objects

____

____

____

potential energy—the amount of energy a thing has because of its position

____

____

____

amount—a quantity of something

____

____

Name: ____________________

I See Energy

Directions: What are some examples of potential and kinetic energy from your daily life? Complete the diary entry below with your examples.

Dear Diary,

Every day, I can see examples of potential and kinetic energy. This morning, I saw three things at school that were examples of potential energy. They were...

During recess, I saw three things that were examples of kinetic energy. They were...

Potential and kinetic energy are different because...

Name: ______________________________

Let There Be Light!

Light is the key to life. Without light, Earth would be a cold and lifeless place. Plants and animals need light to live. Plants use the Sun's light to grow, and animals rely on plants for food and oxygen. No matter how you look at it, light is essential.

Light has different sources, such as the Sun and other stars. During a storm, lightning is a source of light, creating bright flashes across the sky. Things that burn, such as candles and campfires, are also sources of light.

Light is a form of **kinetic**, or moving, energy. Light is always moving—there are examples everywhere. At night, when you see the lights of a faraway house, you are witnessing the movement of light from the house to your eye. When light travels, it moves as **light waves**. There are many types of light waves, but only a few are visible to humans.

1. This passage is mainly about ____________.
   - a. the different types of life on Earth, such as plants and animals
   - b. the complex way that light travels from one point to another
   - c. light energy—its impact, sources, and characteristics
   - d. how humans use light to see the world around them

2. Light is an example of ______________________________, or moving, energy.

3. Which of the following is *not* true about light energy?
   - a. It has different sources, such as the Sun and lightning.
   - b. It is an example of potential energy.
   - c. Life on Earth needs it to survive.
   - d. Not all light waves are visible to the human eye.

Name: ______________________________

Light Waves

When we study light, we look at the parts of a light wave. The two main parts of a light wave are its **crest** and **trough**. A light wave's crest is its highest point. A light wave's trough is the lowest point between two crests. When we study the distance between two crests, we are looking at a **wavelength**.

Visible and Invisible Light

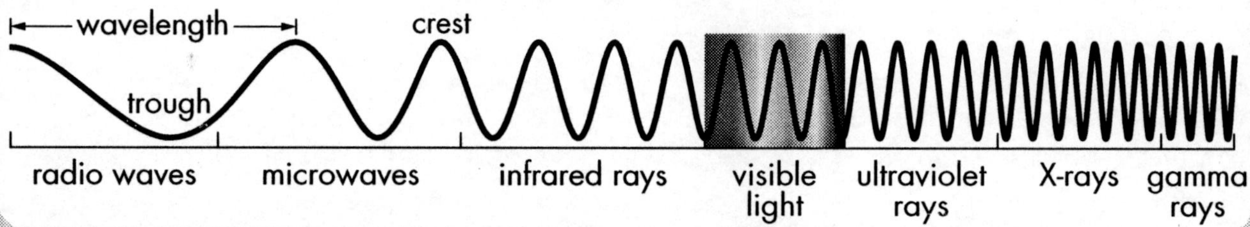

Light wavelengths can be short, medium, or long. Only medium light waves can be seen with the human eye. These waves are called **visible light**. They include all the colors of the rainbow. The colors humans see is determined by wavelength. For instance, the color with the longest wavelength is red light.

Humans cannot see light waves with shorter or longer wavelengths than visible light. **Ultraviolet rays** have short wavelengths. When you get a sunburn, it is because of ultraviolet rays from the Sun.

Light with longer wavelengths includes **infrared rays, microwaves**, and **radio waves**. You can feel the heat of infrared rays, but you cannot see them.

- *Infrared rays* are at work when you turn on a radiator or light a fire.
- *Microwaves* send out phone signals and—you guessed it—power microwave ovens.
- *Radio waves* make radio and television broadcasts possible.

1. How are visible light waves different from those with shorter or longer wavelengths?
   - **a.** Visible light waves can be seen by the human eye.
   - **b.** Visible light waves power phones, radiators, and microwaves.
   - **c.** Examples of visible light waves include ultraviolet light and X-rays.
   - **d.** Visible light waves cause sunburns.

2. The highest point of a light wave is its ______________________________,

   and the lowest point is its ______________________________.

3. Describe light waves with short, visible, and long wavelengths. Include an example of each.

   a. waves shorter than visible light ______________________________

   b. visible light waves ______________________________

   c. waves longer than visible light ______________________________

Name: ______________________________

Word Study—The Power of Light

Directions: Study the diagram below. Then, use each vocabulary word in a sentence that relates to the information from this unit.

Visible and Invisible Light

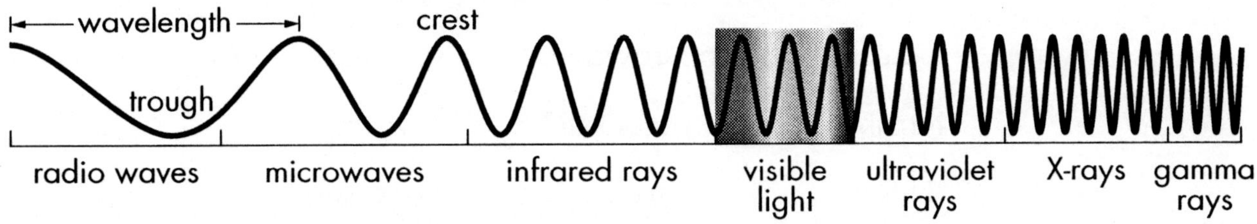

crest—the highest part or point of something (such as a hill or wave)

____

____

____

infrared—producing rays of light that cannot be seen and are *longer* than rays of visible light

____

____

____

trough—the lowest point between two waves or hills

____

____

____

ultraviolet—producing rays of light that cannot be seen and are *shorter* than rays of visible light

____

____

____

wavelength—the distance between two wave crests

____

____

____

Name: ______________________________

Understanding Light Waves

Directions: Complete the sentences with the vocabulary words found in the Word Bank.

Word Bank		
crest	microwaves	trough
infrared	potential	visible
kinetic	radio	wavelength
longer	shorter	waves

1. Light is a form of moving, or ______________________, energy.
2. The highest point of a light wave is called its ______________________.
3. A radiator emits ______________________ rays.
4. Red light has the longest wavelength of ______________________ light.
5. Ultraviolet rays are ______________________ than visible light waves.
6. A ______________________ is the distance between two wave crests.
7. ______________________ waves help broadcast television.
8. Light ______________________ we can see are called visible light.
9. The lowest point between two waves is called a ______________________.
10. Infrared light waves are ______________________ than visible light waves.
11. ______________________ help send phone calls.
12. Light is not an example of stored, or ______________________, energy.

Name: ______________________________

My Science Blog—Light Energy

Directions: Write a blog post about light energy. Your post should include details about visible light waves and light waves that are longer or shorter than visible light. Remember to add a title to your post.

____
(Title)

Visible and Invisible Light

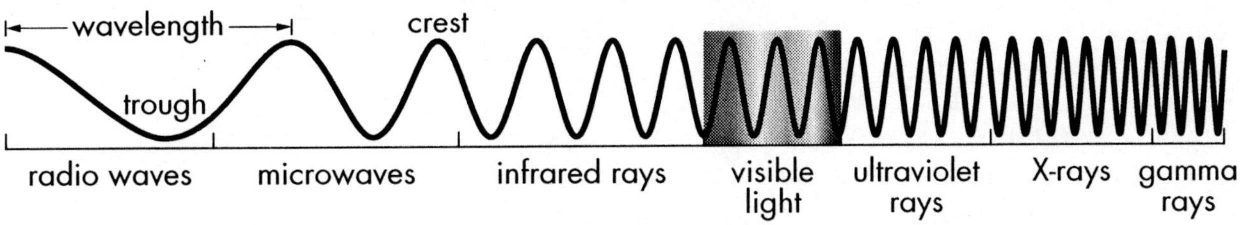

Light is a form of energy. Here are three facts about light.

1. First, light is ____

____

2. ____

____

3. ____

____

There are different types of light waves:

Light waves with wavelengths shorter than visible light ______________________

____

Light waves that we can see ____

____

Light waves with wavelengths longer than visible light ______________________

____

Name: ________________________________

All About Sound

Sound is everywhere. We can hear things close and far—the whisper of a friend or the shout of a coach across the playing field. The loudness of sound is called its **intensity**. Some sounds have a high **pitch** like a bird's chirping song. Others have a low pitch like a bass guitar.

In some ways, sound energy is similar to light energy. Both are found all around us. Both are forms of moving, or **kinetic**, energy. However, light travels far faster than sound. Light can move at 186,282 miles per second. The speed of sound depends on the substance it is passing through. Sound moves faster through water than it does through air. Depending on the temperature of the air, sound moves around 1,100 feet per second. In the water, sound moves around 4,800 feet per second.

Sound moves the fastest in solid material like iron, wood, and stone. When traveling through stone, sound can move at about 19,700 feet per second. But even at this **speed,** sound travels far slower than light!

Like light, sound travels in waves. These sound waves are created when an object **vibrates**. For instance, when you speak or hum, your vocal chords vibrate. These vibrations produce sound waves. Then, these sound waves pass through a substance of some kind. This substance might be water, air, or physical objects. Then, our ears take in these sound waves and transform them into signals. Our brains interpret these signals as different sounds. This is the process that allows us to hear anything!

1. Sound waves are created when an object ______________________.
2. How is sound energy *not* similar to light energy? Circle your answer.
    - **a.** Sound is an example of moving, or kinetic, energy.
    - **b.** Sound moves in waves.
    - **c.** Sound moves in the air at about 1,100 feet per second.
    - **d.** Sound is all around us.
3. Use complete sentences to describe how sound is created.

____

____

____

____

____

Name: ______________________________

Light and Sound

Directions: Study these facts about light and sound energy. Use the facts to complete the *Light vs. Sound* Venn diagram on the following page.

Fast Facts

❍ Plants and animals need light to survive.

❍ Sound can travel at 1,100 feet per second.

❍ Our eyes take in light waves and change them into signals our brains read as different images.

❍ Sound can have a high or a low pitch.

❍ The Sun is an important source of light.

❍ Light and heat energy are often found together, such as in burning objects.

❍ Sound is a form of kinetic energy.

❍ Sound waves happen when an object vibrates.

❍ The colors we see are determined by the wavelength of light.

❍ Light can travel at 186,282 miles per second.

❍ The intensity of sound can be loud or soft.

❍ The faster an object vibrates, the higher its pitch will be.

❍ Light is a form of kinetic energy.

❍ Our ears take in sound waves and change them into signals our brains read as different sounds.

❍ The stronger an object vibrates, the louder the sound will be.

Name: ______________________________

Light and Sound *(cont.)*

Directions: Compare *light* and *sound*. How are they different? How are they similar? Write at least three facts in each section of the Venn diagram.

Light

1. ______________________________
2. ______________________________
3. ______________________________

Both

1. ______________________________
2. ______________________________
3. ______________________________

Sound

1. ______________________________
2. ______________________________
3. ______________________________

Name: ______________________________

Underwater Waves

The ocean is filled with sound. Some of the world's greatest chatterboxes live in the ocean! One of these creatures is the bottlenose dolphin.

Dolphins talk to one another using squeaks and whistles. Some of these sounds are very high-pitched. Humans are not able to hear them. Dolphins use sound to locate objects that are far away. This process is called **echolocation**.

Echolocation is powerful. Dolphins can use it to learn the size and shape of an object. They do so by making clicking noises, which create sound waves. These sound waves move through the water and bounce off objects. When the sound waves bounce, they create echoes.

Dolphins can read sound-wave echoes to learn more about an object. They use the echoes to tell how far away an object is and how fast it is moving. Echolocation is a form of **sonar**. Sonar includes anything that uses sound waves to locate objects under water. Humans use sonar for many things. We use it to locate different objects in the ocean, such as shipwrecks. Sonar can also be used to map the ocean floor!

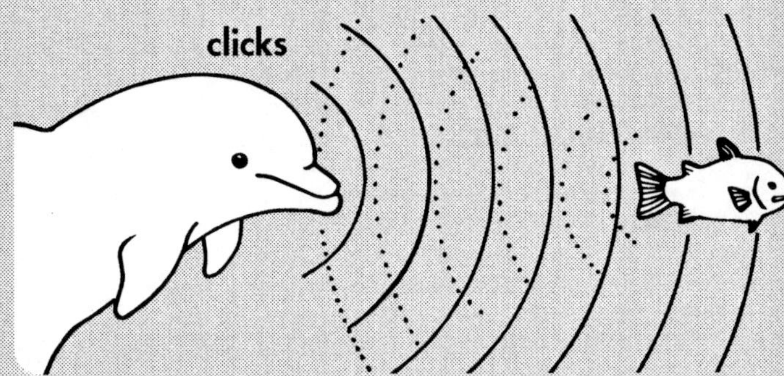

Sound-wave echoes tell dolphins the size, shape, distance, speed, and location of different underwater objects.

1. Put the steps of dolphin *echolocation* in order 1–5. The first one has been done for you.

   ______ When the sound waves bounce, they create echoes that the dolphin reads.

   __1__ A dolphin makes a clicking noise.

   ______ These sound waves bounce off objects under water.

   ______ The clicking noise creates sound waves.

   ______ A dolphin uses the echoes to learn the object's size, shape, distance, speed, and location.

2. How is dolphin *echolocation* similar to the *sonar* humans use?
   - **a.** Both use whistles, squeaks, and clicks.
   - **b.** Both use sound waves to locate objects.
   - **c.** Both create sounds that can be heard by all animals.
   - **d.** Both are used to locate objects on land and under water.

3. What can dolphins learn about an object by using *echolocation*?

____

____

____

Name: ____

Dolphin Echolocation

Directions: Think about how dolphins use sound. Use the pictures below to help you describe the process of echolocation.

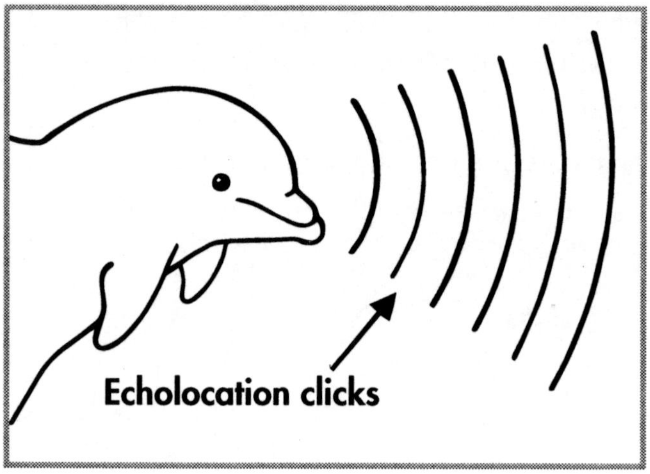

First, ____

____

____

____

____

____

____

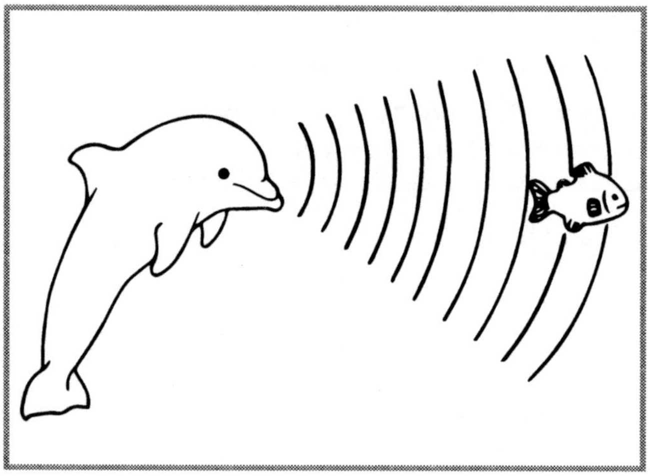

Then, ____

____

____

____

____

____

____

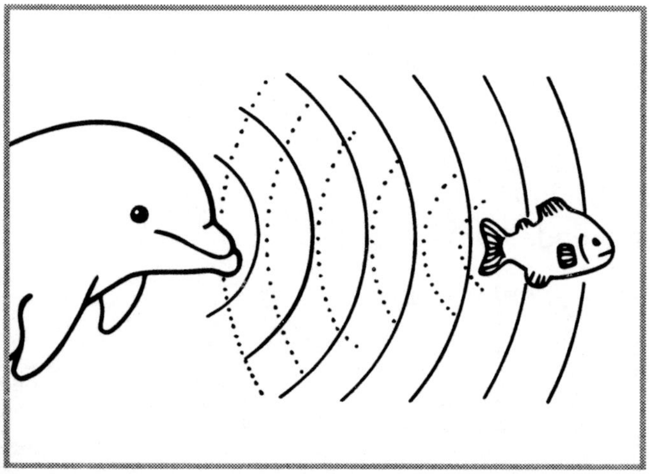

Finally, ____

____

____

____

____

____

____

Name: ______________________________

Word Study—The "How" of Sound

Directions: Read and study the following vocabuary words and definitions. Then, use each vocabulary word in a sentence that relates to the information from this unit.

echolocation—the process of using sound waves to locate distant objects

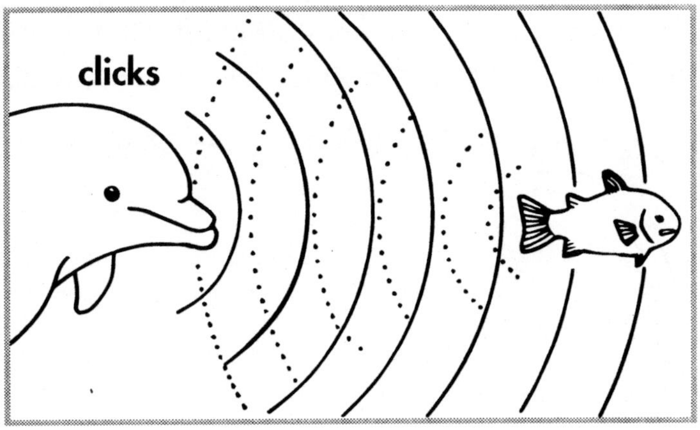

____

____

____

____

____

intensity—when related to sound, it describes how soft or loud a sound is

____

____

____

pitch—when related to sound, it describes how low or high a sound is

____

____

____

sonar—anything that uses sound waves to locate objects under water

____

____

____

vibrates—moves back and forth or from side to side with very short, quick movements

____

____

____

Name: ______________________________

A Dolphin Tale

Directions: Write a story about a bottlenose dolphin exploring the ocean using **echolocation**.

Remember: Dolphins use echolocation by making clicking noises that create sound waves. These sound waves bounce off objects in the water and create echoes. Dolphins read these echoes and learn more about the size, shape, distance, location, and speed of objects.

Name: ______________________________

Changes in Energy

We know that energy has many forms. There is *light*, *heat*, and *sound* energy. There is also *chemical* and *electrical* energy.

Energy can change from one form to another. This is called an **energy conversion**. It happens all the time.

- Picture a plant on a sunny day. The plant is taking in the Sun's light. It converts this **light energy** into food. The food is a form of **chemical energy**. This is a type of stored energy. Chemical energy is found in many places. It is found in food, engines, and batteries.
- Now, picture a dark forest. You only have a flashlight to guide the way. When you click on the flashlight, conversions take place. The flashlight's battery has chemical energy. When the flashlight is turned on, this chemical energy changes into electrical energy as it passes through the wires. The electrical energy is then converted into light energy. This creates a beam of light!

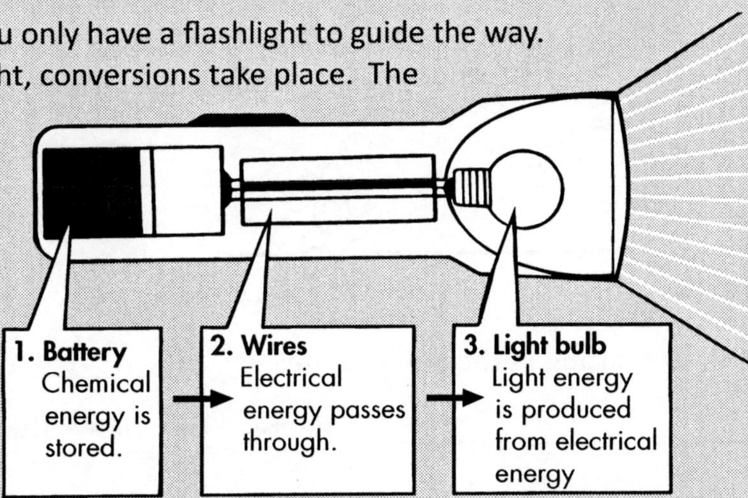

1. What does the word *conversion* mean?
   a. working by means of chemicals
   b. a chance that something will happen in the future
   c. the act or process of changing from one form to another
   d. a device that is placed inside machines to supply it with electricity
2. Which of the following is *not* true about *chemical energy*?
   a. It is a form of stored energy.
   b. Chemical energy can only be converted into light energy.
   c. It can be found in batteries.
   d. We use food as a source of chemical energy.
3. When energy changes forms, it is called an energy ______________________________.
4. Describe an example of an *energy conversion* from your daily life.

____

____

____

Name: ______________________________

Energy Conversions

Directions: Think about how energy converts from one form to another. Study the images. Then complete the sentences with words from the Word Bank. Each word should only be used once.

Word Bank		
chemical	electrical	light
conversion	heat	sound

1.

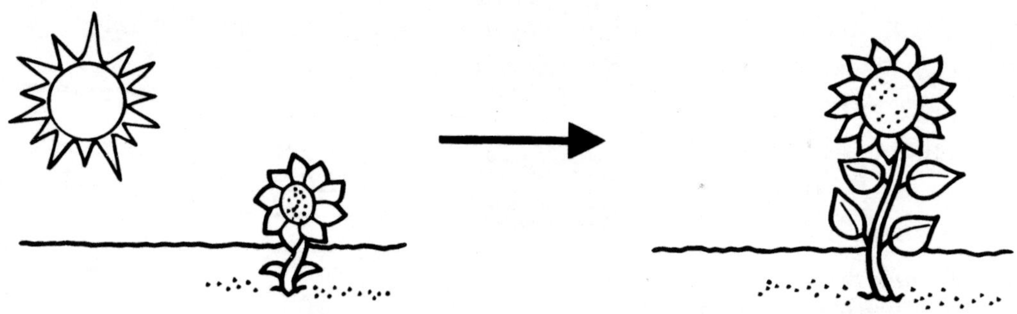

A flower sitting in the Sun changes ____________________ energy into food, or ____________________ energy. This allows the flower to grow.

2.

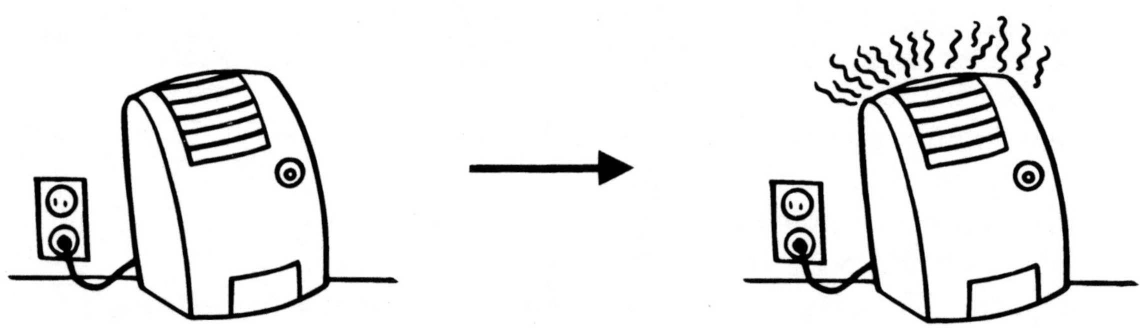

When you plug in a heater, you are changing ____________________ energy into ____________________ energy.

3.

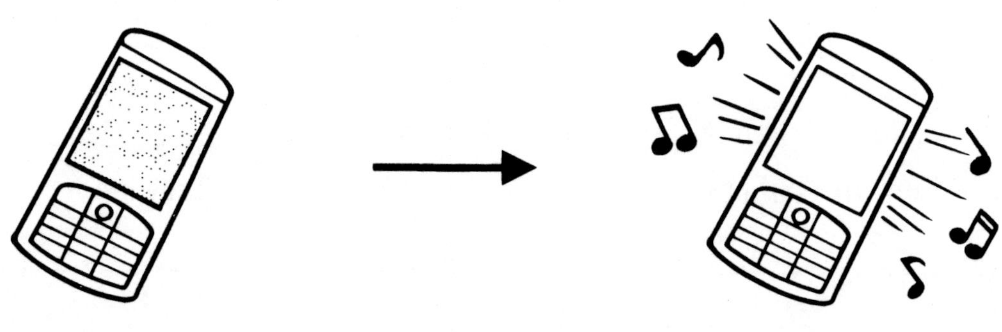

A phone ringing is an example of a ____________________ from electrical energy to ____________________ energy.

Name: ______________________________

Word Study—
Energy: Conversions and Collisions

Directions: Study the definitions. Then, use each vocabulary word in a sentence that relates to the information from this unit.

conversion—the act or process of changing from one form to another

____

____

____

chemical energy—a type of stored energy found in many places such as food, engines, and batteries

____

____

____

electrical energy—a form of energy resulting from the flow of an electrical charge

____

____

____

light—the form of energy that makes it possible to see things

____

____

____

transfer—move or shift from one place to another

____

____

____

Name: ______________________________

Crash! Boom! Pow!

Annie was driving her car. Ahead, she saw the car in front of her stop suddenly. She tried to swerve out of the way, but it was too late. Her car slammed into the other car, pushing it across the street.

Luckily, Annie and the other driver were not hurt. The cars were a different story. Annie's front fender had been twisted. The hood of her car was crushed. The other driver's rear end had been completely smashed. Both cars were wrecked.

In a crash like Annie's, there is an energy **transfer** between cars. When the cars collide, they transfer kinetic energy, causing each car to change its direction. In other words, when Annie's car crashed into the other car, it stopped her car from moving forward and pushed the other car forward.

Car accident

During collisions between objects, energy can also transfer into the air. This may be heat or sound energy. That is why a car crash is loud. The collision of two cars releases sound energy into the air.

1. Which of the following is an example of a *collision*?
   - **a.** a top spinning on a flat surface
   - **b.** two dogs running side by side
   - **c.** a squirrel climbing a tree
   - **d.** a golf club hitting a golf ball
2. When two objects collide, there is a ______________________ of energy between the objects.
3. Use complete sentences to describe what happens when two objects collide.

____

____

____

____

____

Name: ______________________________

Energy at Work: Baseball

Directions: Think about energy at work in a baseball game. What are examples of energy *conversions*? What are examples of energy *collisions*? Use the Word Bank to help you respond to the statements below.

Word Bank		
chemical energy	electric energy	light energy
collision	heat energy	sound energy
conversion	kinetic energy	transfer

1. Describe what happens to energy when a player hits a baseball with a bat.

____

____

____

____

2. Describe what happens to energy when a player runs across a field to catch a ball.

____

____

____

____

3. Describe what happens to energy when night-game lights are turned on.

____

____

____

____

Name: ____________________________________

Natural Wonder

Imagine you are lying on the beach, staring out at the ocean. You carefully watch the water move back and forth across the sandy shore. Some waves are small and gentle. Others are gigantic waves that make great crashing sounds when they hit the shore.

Waves are natural wonders that are most frequently created by the wind. Far away from the shore, wind hits the water. As the wind makes its impact, water shifts, creating waves.

When scientists study waves, they study their different parts. The two main parts of a wave are its **crest** and **trough**. A wave's crest is its highest point. A wave's trough is the lowest point between two crests. When scientists study the distance between two crests, they are studying the wave's **wavelength**.

Lying on the beach is an opportunity for scientific discovery! Next time you are at the beach, inspect the parts of a wave:

- ↑ How high are each wave's crests?
- ↓ How low are its troughs?
- ↔ Can you estimate the wavelength of each wave?

1. Circle the two details that support the following main idea.

Main Idea **Waves are caused by the wind.**

Detail 1: When wind hits the surface of the water, water is shifted.

Detail 2: A wave's trough is the lowest point between two crests.

Detail 3: The stronger the wind, the more energy in the waves.

Detail 4: Some waves are small and gentle.

2. Which of the following correctly describes a *wavelength*?

- **a.** the highest part of a wave
- **b.** the distance between a crest and a trough
- **c.** the distance between two crests
- **d.** the lowest part of a wave

3. Use complete sentences to describe the difference between a wave's *crest* and its *trough*.

____

____

____

____

Name: ______________________________

Waves Are Natural Wonders

Directions: Study the diagram below. Then, answer the questions.

Dimensions of a Wave of Water

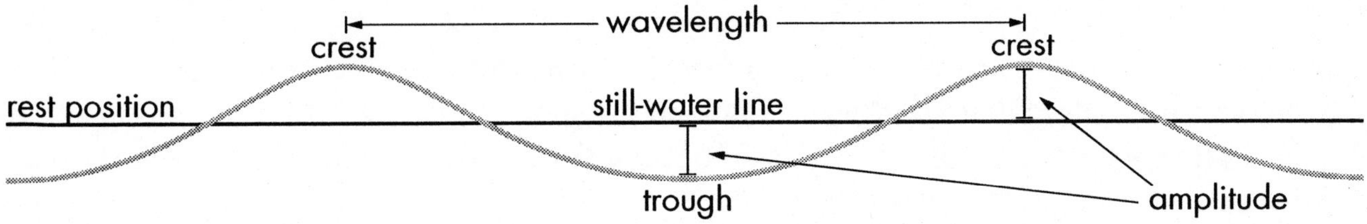

1. How is a *wavelength* measured?

____

____

2. Judging from the diagram, a wave's *amplitude* is found by measuring from the *still-water line* (rest position) to the ______________ or the ______________.

3. How does the diagram help you understand the parts of a wave?

____

____

____

4. Draw a series of waves in the box below. Label each wave's *crests* and *troughs*. Label one *wavelength* and one *amplitude*.

Name: ______________________________

Deadly Waves

One of the deadliest natural disasters is just three syllables. Its name is **tsunami** (soo-NAH-me). In the past, these waves have caused major havoc. They have killed thousands of people and destroyed many landforms.

Tsunamis are like race cars—they speed dangerously across the ocean. Deep-water waves can move over 400 miles per hour! Once they reach the shore, these waves can be monstrous in height. The height of a wave is called its **amplitude**. In 2004, a tsunami in the Indian Ocean had waves with amplitudes of 30 feet!

So, how are these deadly waves created? Unlike most waves, tsunamis are not usually caused by the wind. In many cases, they are caused by huge earthquakes. But such earthquakes do not occur on land. Instead, these great quakes happen under water.

When earthquakes occur, they create a lot of energy. The floor of the ocean shifts and shakes. This makes the water move. In other words, the energy created by the earthquake is transferred to the water. The result of this energy transfer is huge, deadly waves!

1. What does the word *transferred* likely mean in the statement "the energy created by the earthquake is transferred"?
   - **a.** to move to a higher position
   - **b.** to separate into parts by pulling
   - **c.** to move something from one place to another
   - **d.** to develop or form over time

2. The height of a wave is called its __________.
   - **a.** amplitude
   - **b.** tsunami
   - **c.** trough
   - **d.** transfer
3. Which of the following is *not* true about *tsunamis*?
   - **a.** Their waves have large amplitudes.
   - **b.** Many tsunamis are caused by earthquakes.
   - **c.** Energy from the water is transferred to the ocean floor, causing earthquakes.
   - **d.** Tsunamis are destructive forces that can damage whole communities.
4. Use complete sentences to describe how tsunamis are created by earthquakes.

____

____

____

____

Name: ______________________________

Word Study—The Wonder of Waves

Directions: Think about what you have learned about waves. Match each sentence starter with its correct ending.

_______ **1.** The height of a wave is

_______ **2.** The distance between two wave crests is

_______ **3.** A wave's *crest* is

_______ **4.** A wave's *trough* is

_______ **5.** Many tsunamis are

_______ **6.** Tsunamis have

(a) its highest point.

(b) killed thousands and destroyed landforms.

(c) called its *amplitude*.

(d) caused by huge earthquakes.

(e) called a *wavelength*.

(f) the lowest point between two crests.

Label It! Use the words in the Word Bank to correctly label the graphic below.

Word Bank
amplitude
crest
trough
wavelength

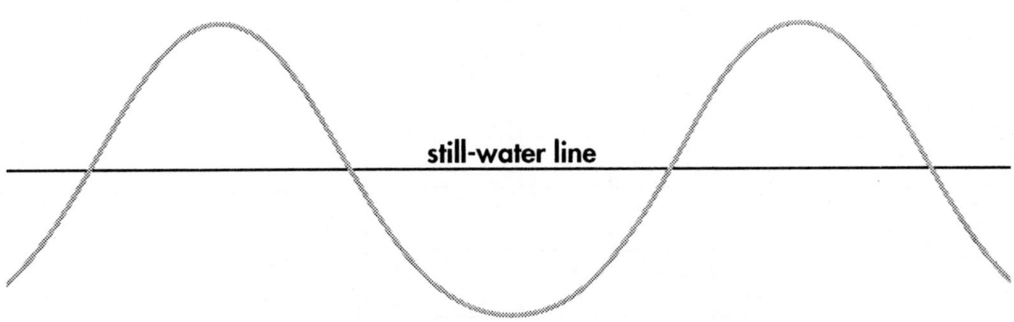

Name: ______________________________

Writing the Waves

Directions: Imagine you are a news reporter. You are writing an article about waves. Your article should include details about the parts of a wave as well as information related to tsunamis. Remember to write a headline for your article and a caption for your drawing.

The Wave Reporter

Writer: ______________________________ **Date:** ______________

____

____

(headline)

Caption: ______________________________

Name: ______________________________

Eye Spy

For humans, without light, there is no sight! Light allows us to see objects big and small. Light reflects off objects before entering our eyes. The way light reflects gives objects their color and shape.

Vision is a complex process. When light first enters the eye, it passes through the **cornea**. The cornea is a protective layer that helps the eye focus. After the cornea, light moves through the **pupil**. The pupil is the opening at the center of the eye.

The pupil is surrounded by the colored **iris**. When you say a person has blue eyes, you are referring to the color of their irises. The iris can change in size. When the iris opens larger, more light is let in. When the iris closes, less light is let in.

The **lens** of the eye is directly behind the iris. The lens changes shape depending on the distance of the object. The lens flattens to focus on distant objects. The lens thickens to focus on close objects. After passing through the lens, light moves through the center of the eye and on to the **retina**. The retina has special cells that take in the focused light and turn it into signals.

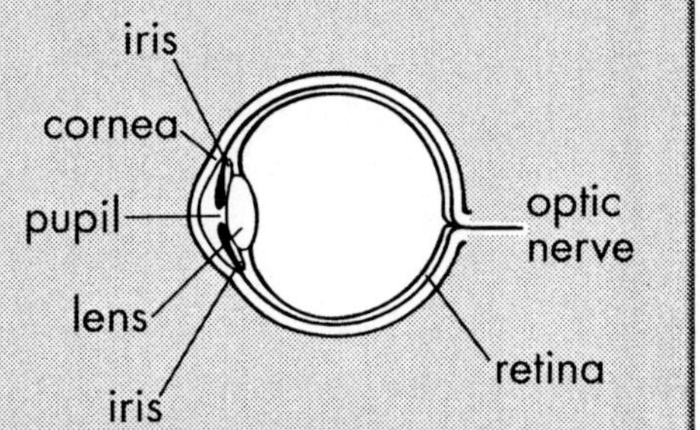

The signals are sent to the brain through the **optic nerve**. The brain sees the signals as an image. This is how the many parts of the eye work together to create sight!

1. What does the word *reflects* mean in the statement "Light reflects off objects before entering our eyes"?

   a. causes **b.** pierces **c.** bounces **d.** control

2. Check two facts about the eye's lens.

   ☐ **Fact 1:** The lens changes shape based on the distance of an object.

   ☐ **Fact 2:** Light first enters the lens, which acts as a protective layer.

   ☐ **Fact 3:** When looking at a close object, the lens thickens.

   ☐ **Fact 4:** The lens is an opening at the center of the eye.

3. Think about the process of sight. Put the steps in order 1–7. The first one has been done for you.

   ____ Then, the light passes through the pupil, the opening at the center of the eye.
   __1__ Light first enters the eye through the cornea, a protective layer.
   ____ Light then moves through the center of the eye and on to the retina.
   ____ Special cells in the retina turn the focused light into signals.
   ____ Next, light enters the lens, which changes shape depending on the position of an object.
   ____ Finally, the brain sees the signals as an image.
   ____ Then, the signals are sent to the brain through the optic nerve.

Name: ______________________________

In the Eye

Directions: Study the diagram. Then, complete the sentences with the vocabulary words found in the Word Bank.

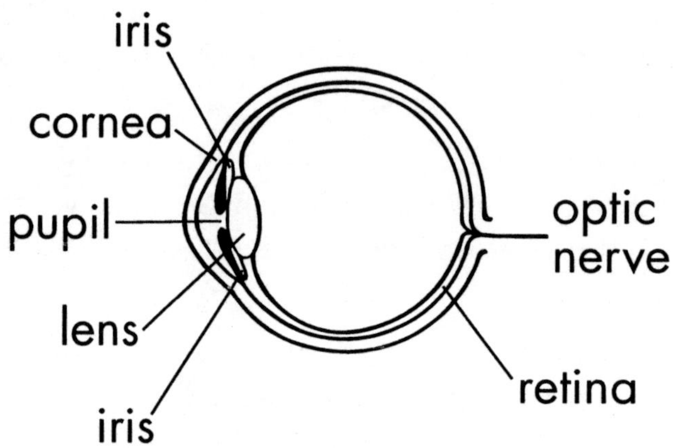

Word Bank		
cornea	lens	pupil
iris	light	retina

1. The ______________________ has special cells that turn focused light into signals the brain sees as images.

2. ______________________ reflects off objects, giving them their color and shape.

3. When viewing a distant object, the ______________________ flattens.

4. The ______________________ is a protective layer that helps the eye focus.

5. Directly in front of the lens, the ______________________ can change in size.

6. The ______________________ is the opening at the center of the eye.

Name: ____________________

Seeing in the Dark

It's the middle of the night. You are very thirsty. You get out of bed and head to the kitchen. Halfway there, you stumble over a chair. You are so startled you yell! Sound familiar? Human eyes don't see that well in the dark. This is not the case for all creatures. Some animals, like the gecko, see best at night.

Many gecko species are **nocturnal**, which means they are most active at night. Like most nocturnal creatures, the structure of their eyes allows them to see well in the dark. The structure of a gecko's eye is different from the structure of a human eye.

One of the reasons nocturnal creatures see better in the dark is that their eyes can take in more light. When there is little light, the pupils of the gecko open wider. Geckos also have more of the eye cells that allow them to see better in the dark. Their eyes can see color clearly at night! This makes their eyes extremely sensitive to light.

In order to protect their eyes, geckos have slit-like pupils. These pupils are able to close quickly when faced with bright light. Many other nocturnal creatures have these same eye structures.

1. What does *nocturnal* mean?

   a. knock over **b.** knowledgeable **c.** active at night **d.** active in trees

2. Circle the two causes that match the following effect.

Effect	Geckos are able to see better than humans at night.

   Cause 1: They are more active at night.

   Cause 2: They have more eye cells that allow them to see color at night.

   Cause 3: They have slit-like pupils that close quickly.

   Cause 4: Their pupils open wider when there is little light.

3. How are the eyes of *nocturnal* creatures different from human eyes?

   ____

   ____

   ____

   ____

Name: ______________________________

Word Study—Light and Sight

Directions: Study the definitions. Then, use each vocabulary word in a sentence that relates to the information from this unit.

cornea—the clear outer covering of the eye, which protects the eye and helps it focus

____

____

____

lens—the part of the eye that changes shape depending on the position of the object, flattening to focus on distant objects and thickening to focus on close objects

____

____

____

nocturnal—active mainly at night

____

____

____

pupil—the round opening at the center of the eye, surrounded by the colored iris

____

____

____

retina—the sensitive tissue at the back of the eye that receives images and sends signals to the brain about what is seen

____

____

____

Name: ______________________________

Is Light Important?

Directions: Think about how humans and other creatures see. Does light have an important role? Why or why not? Include reasons that support your opinion in your response.

Name: ______________________________

The Wonders of the Human Brain

Our brains are complex and powerful. They are in charge of our thoughts and feelings. Our brains control how we experience the world. To understand the brain, we must understand its structure.

The human brain has three main parts:

- The largest part of the brain is called the **cerebrum**. When you are eating a meal or watching a movie, the cerebrum is at work. It is in charge of the five senses: sight, smell, touch, taste, and sound. It is also in charge of many other things. The cerebrum controls emotions, thinking, memory, and **personality**.
- The **brain stem** is another part of the brain. It is found at the brain's base. The brain stem connects to the **spinal cord**. It is responsible for the things you don't think about, like breathing, heartbeat, or body temperature.
- The third part of the brain is called the **cerebellum**. It is found between the cerebrum and the brain stem. The cerebellum is in charge of muscle activity as well as balance.

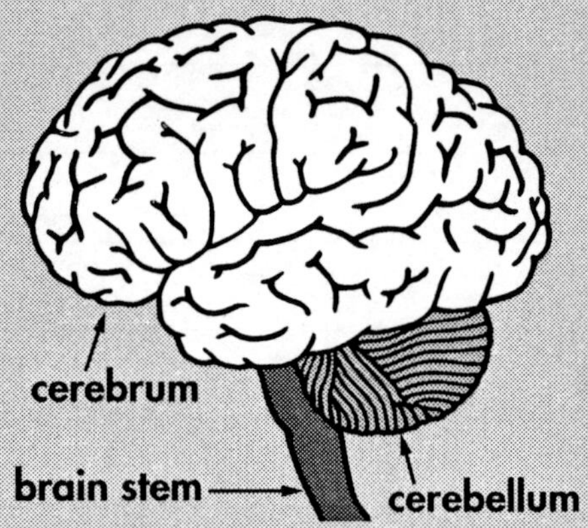

1. The structure of the brain has three parts. What are they?

   1. ______________________________
   2. ______________________________
   3. ______________________________

2. Which of the following is an example of the *cerebellum* at work?
   - **a.** A young gymnast balances carefully on a high beam.
   - **b.** Two friends sing along to their favorite song.
   - **c.** A boy smells pizza cooking in the kitchen.
   - **d.** The basketball player's heart thumps steadily.

3. Which of the following is the *cerebrum* not in charge of?
   - **a.** processing how something tastes
   - **b.** feelings and memories
   - **c.** breathing and body temperature
   - **d.** processing how something looks

4. In your opinion, what is the most powerful part of the brain? Why?

____

____

____

Name: ______________________________

The Three Parts of the Brain

Directions: Study the diagram below. Then, respond to the questions using complete sentences.

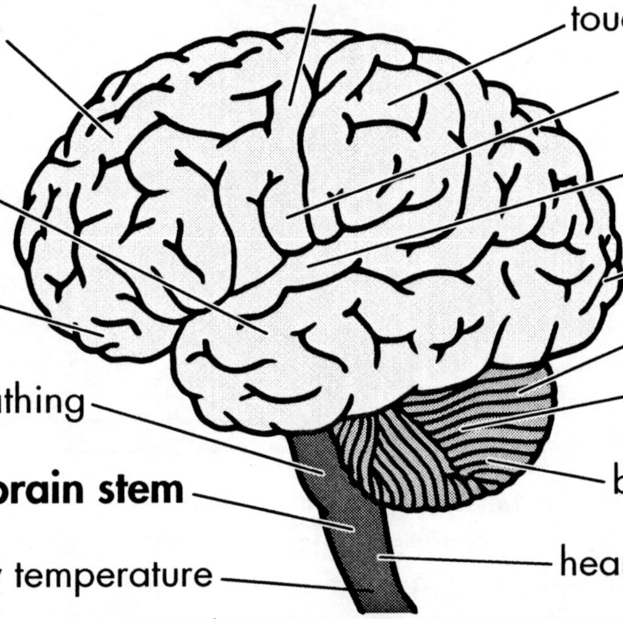

1. Provide two examples of when the *cerebrum* is at work.

____

____

____

____

2. Provide two examples of when the *cerebellum* is at work.

____

____

____

____

3. Provide two examples of when the *brain stem* is at work.

____

____

____

____

Name: ______________________________

A Day in the Great Outdoors

It is a scorching hot day in the middle of summer. You flinch at the heat of the Sun on your skin as you walk through the forest. "I should have brought sunscreen," you mumble to yourself.

During your walk, you inspect familiar plants and try to remember their names. You are lost in thought when you hear a low rumble. In the distance, you see a terrifying sight—a giant grizzly bear on its hind legs. The bear gives a **thunderous** roar!

In a second, you are moving. You can feel your heartbeat as you jump over boulders and dive through bushes. Finally, you see a wide, rushing river.

Across the surging river is a large, fallen log. The log doesn't look nearly stable enough to walk across, but you must take your chances. Balancing on the wobbly log, you look over your shoulder. The bear is much closer. You put one foot in front of the other and in a few minutes, you are on the other side.

The bear starts across the log, but the log slips from its place, and the bear falls. It roars with frustration. You can barely breathe. Against all odds, you made it to safety!

1. When the person in the story balances on the wobbly log, what part of the brain is at work?
   - **a.** the brain stem
   - **b.** the cerebrum
   - **c.** the cerebellum

2. What does the word *thunderous* likely mean?
   - **a.** frequently seen
   - **b.** very loud
   - **c.** to attack or move forward
   - **d.** a feeling of annoyance

3. Which of the following does not show activity of the *cerebrum*, the part of the brain that controls memory and the senses?
   - **a.** hearing a low rumble
   - **b.** seeing a grizzly bear
   - **c.** trying to remember a plant's name
   - **d.** breathing

4. How do our brains help us survive?

____

____

____

____

Name: ______________________________

Word Study—The Human Brain

Directions: Study the definitions. Then, use each vocabulary word in a sentence that relates to the information from this unit.

brain stem—connected to the spinal cord; in charge of such things as breathing, heartbeat, and body temperature

____

____

____

cerebellum—found between the cerebrum and the brain stem; in charge of such things as muscle activity and balance

____

____

____

cerebrum—the largest part of the brain; in charge of such things as the five senses, emotions, thinking, memory, and personality

____

____

____

personality—a set of emotional qualities that makes one person different from another person

____

____

____

spinal cord—the large group of nerves which runs through the center of the spine and carries messages between the brain and the rest of the body

____

____

____

Name: ______________________________

The Power of the Brain

Directions: Complete the chart below. Describe how each part of your brain is key to survival. Write at least three facts for each part of the brain.

Cerebrum

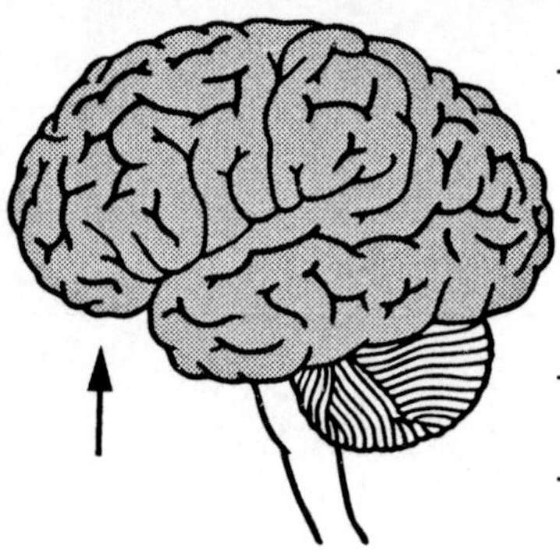

Cerebellum

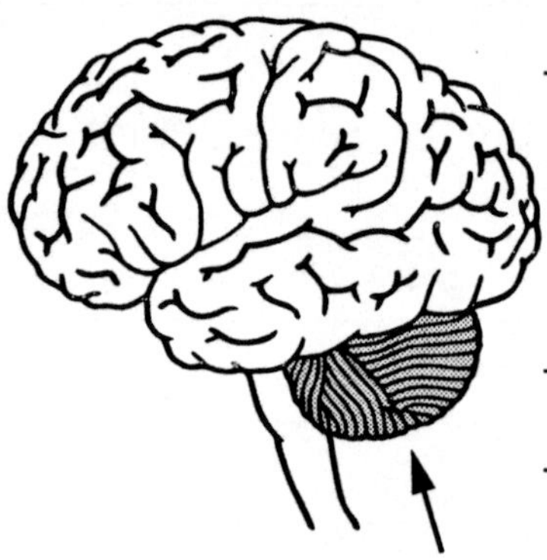

Brain Stem

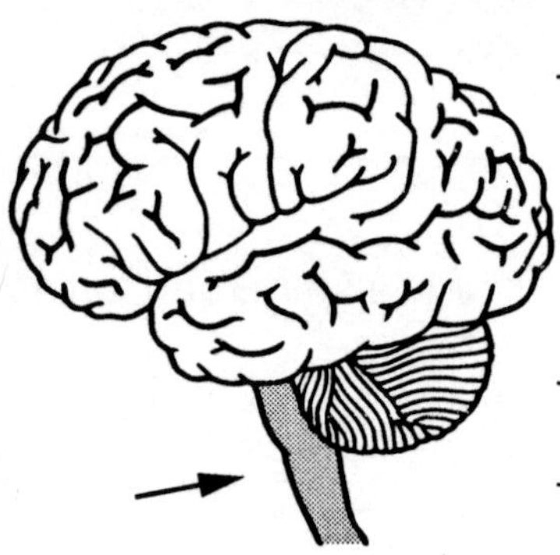

Name: ______________________________

Fennec Foxes—Tiny but Tough

Surviving in the desert is no easy feat. Desert **ecosystems** have extreme weather. Days can be scorching hot or freezing cold. Deserts occur anywhere there is low rainfall and little wildlife.

Desert creatures have unique features that help them **survive**. The fennec fox is one such creature. This small fox is known for its giant ears. The fox's ears are almost half the size of its entire body! The fennec fox's large ears are an **adaptation** that allows it to flourish in its desert **habitat**.

A fennec fox can hear its prey even when it cannot see it. Its large ears allow it to hear creatures crawling underground. It uses this special skill to catch insects, rodents, and other small creatures.

Its ears also help it stay cool. The fox's ears release heat. A fennec fox can use its ears to cool down even in the hottest weather.

1. This text is mainly about ________________.
   a. how deserts are places with low rainfall and little wildlife
   b. how a fennec fox uses its unique adaptation to survive in a tough habitat
   c. how fennec foxes are at the top of the desert food chain
   d. how the desert has extreme weather in every season
2. What does the word *adaptation* likely mean?
   a. a change in a plant or animal that makes it better able to live in a particular place
   b. an interesting or important part, quality, or ability
   c. to allow to enter the air, water, or soil
   d. everything that exists in a particular environment
3. Which of the following does *not* describe desert ecosystems?
   a. an ecosystem that can have extremely hot or cold weather
   b. ecosystems that suffer from spring and summer floods
   c. a dry place where it rarely rains
   d. an ecosystem with little wildlife
4. How do the ears of a fennec fox help it *survive* in its extreme environment?

____

____

____

Name: ______________________________

Survival in the Desert

Directions: Read the main idea. Then, write details that support the main idea in the boxes below.

Main Idea A fennec fox's ears help it survive in the desert.

Supporting Detail 1:

Supporting Detail 2:

Supporting Detail 3:

Name: ______________________________

The Sneaky Sidewinder

Meet one of the desert's sneakiest creatures! It is called the sidewinder snake. Like the fennec fox, the sidewinder has many adaptations that help it thrive in hot, sandy deserts.

This snake was named for its creative way of getting around. It moves sideways across the sand. When on the move, the snake only touches the sand with a small part of its body at a time. This helps the snake keep itself from getting too hot.

So, why is the sidewinder sneaky? The snake is like an undercover agent. It surprises its prey. When hunting, the sidewinder buries itself under the sand. The snake only keeps its eyes above ground. The snake's light-colored and spotted body blends in with the sand. This camouflages the snake and helps it **ambush** its prey.

1. What does the word *ambush* likely mean?
   - **a.** to make very little noise
   - **b.** an animal that is hunted by another animal
   - **c.** a surprise attack
   - **d.** to struggle in physical combat
2. Which of the following statements best summarizes the passage?
   - **a.** The sidewinder has many adaptations that help it thrive in hot, sandy deserts.
   - **b.** By decreasing its contact with the sand, the snake keeps itself from getting too hot.
   - **c.** Meet one of the desert's sneakiest creatures!
   - **d.** The snake is like an undercover agent.
3. The author uses the word *sneaky* to describe the sidewinder because the snake ________.
   - **a.** is designed for its habitat
   - **b.** buries itself under the sand and ambushes its prey
   - **c.** moves sideways across the sand
   - **d.** only touches the sand with a small part of its body

4. In your opinion, what makes the sidewinder "designed" for its habitat?

____

____

____

____

Name: ______________________________

Word Study—Surviving in the Wild

Directions: Study the definitions. Then, use each vocabulary word in a sentence that relates to the information from this unit.

adaptation—a change in a plant or an animal that makes it better able to live in a particular place

ambush—to attack someone or something by surprise from a hidden place

ecosystem—everything that exists in a particular environment

habitat—the place where a plant or an animal normally lives or grows

survive—to continue to live in spite of danger or hardship

Name: ______________________________

Adapting to the Desert

Directions: Think about how the fennec fox and the sidewinder snake have adapted to their environment. How have their adaptations allowed them to overcome the challenges of living in the desert?

Fennec Fox	Sidewinder Snake
Desert Challenge 1: Heat	**Desert Challenge 1: Heat**
Desert Challenge 2: Finding Food	**Desert Challenge 2: Finding Food**

Name: ____________________________________

Groups in the Wild

Friends and family are important to humans. We like to be part of a group. We often spend time in groups and look out for those who are close to us. Animals are no different. Animals also spend time together and look out for one another.

Living in a family or a group can make survival in the wild more likely, but not every animal group is the same. Some groups are large. Others are small. Some groups are always on the move. Others like to stay in one place. The way animals **behave** in a group not only helps them survive, but also gives them a chance to **reproduce** and start families of their own.

Chickens

There are some animal groups that have a **hierarchy**. This means that one or more animals in the group are in charge. These are called **dominant** animals. These animals show their dominance in different ways. They may get the first pick of food, shelter, or mates. They may also show their dominance by protecting the rest of the group. Gorillas, wolves, and chickens are all examples of animals that live in a hierarchy.

1. Animal groups with *dominant* members have a ______________________________.

2. Which of the following is true of animal groups? Circle your answer.
   - **a.** Most animal groups have over 10 members.
   - **b.** Living in groups can make animals more likely to survive.
   - **c.** Larger animals are more likely to live in a hierarchy.
   - **d.** Most animals use the same behavior to survive.

3. What do you think may be some of the benefits of living in a *hierarchy*?

____

____

____

____

Name: ______________________________

Understanding Animal Groups

Directions: Think about what you have learned about animal groups. Match each sentence starter with its correct ending.

_______ **1.** Living in a group can increase

_______ **2.** Animal groups with hierarchies

_______ **3.** Animals may show their dominance by

(a) getting first pick of food and shelter.

(b) an animal's chances of survival.

(c) have dominant members who are in charge.

Word Study—Animal Groups

Directions: Study the following vocabulary words and definitions. Then, use each vocabulary word in a sentence that relates to the information from this unit.

behave—to act in a particular way

____

____

dominant—commanding, controlling, or defeating all others

____

____

hierarchy—a system in which people, animals, or things are placed in a series of levels with different importance or status

____

____

reproduce—to produce babies, young animals, new plants, etc.

____

____

Name: ______________________________

Protecting the Young

Being an animal parent can be tough. Animals have to work hard to make sure their babies survive. Some animals are very devoted to their young. The meerkat is one example of a committed animal parent.

Meerkats live in southern Africa. They make their homes in both grasslands and deserts. Meerkats sleep and hide from predators in **burrows**. These are underground systems of tunnels and chambers. During the day, they look for food, such as insects and other small creatures. Baby meerkats are called **pups**. Pups are looked after by the entire pack. When it is time to search for food, a few adults stay behind in the burrows. They look after the pups.

A few weeks after they are born, pups come out from the burrows. Adult meerkats teach them how to stay safe while above ground. For the next few months, the pups remain **dependent** on adult meerkats. The adults feed and watch over them. Pups need to be protected from **predators**. These include eagles, jackals, and even meerkats from other packs.

1. What does the word *dependent* mean in the sentence, "For the next few months, the pups remain dependent on adult meerkats."?
   - **a.** Adult meerkats are overprotective of pups.
   - **b.** Pups are independent from an early age.
   - **c.** Adult meerkats get tired of taking care of pups.
   - **d.** Pups need care and to learn from adult meerkats.
2. Eagles and jackals are examples of meerkat ______________________________.
3. How does a meerkat's behavior help it survive?

____

____

____

____

Name: ______________________________

Writing About Animal Groups

Directions: Think about animal groups. Use the Word Bank to help you respond to the prompt below.

Word Bank		
behavior	dominant	reproduce
dependent	hierarchy	survival

Prompt How do animals behave in groups? How do certain behaviors help animals survive?

Name: ____________________

Growing Together

Miss Walton's fourth-grade class was like every other fourth-grade class. Well, except for one thing: Miss Walton's class had a beautiful outdoor garden. Every Friday, the students took a short field trip to visit the garden. They were excited to see their growing plants. Some students were competing to see whose plant would grow the fastest! After each visit to the garden, Miss Walton tested her students on their plant knowledge.

"Who knows what plants need to grow?" she asked the class.

"I do!" A student named Sara raised her hand. "Most plants must have water, air, and sunshine in order to grow."

"Good job, Sarah," Miss Walton remarked. "Okay, who can describe **photosynthesis**, the process plants use to make food?"

Sam raised his hand. "I can."

"Go ahead, Sam," Miss Walton said.

"Okay, so the first step in photosynthesis happens when plants **absorb** (take in) sunlight. Plants have a special substance called **chlorophyll**, which absorbs the Sun's energy. Plants also absorb carbon dioxide from the surrounding air and water from the ground. The Sun's energy is used to transform the water and carbon dioxide into sugars. These sugars are used by plants as food."

"Great answer!" Miss Walton cheered. "But we are missing one detail. Does anyone know what it is?"

"Photosynthesis also causes plants to release oxygen," one student called out.

"You got it!" Miss Walton exclaimed.

1. Circle the two causes that match the following effect:

Effect A plant releases oxygen into the air.

Cause 1: Plants are able to create their own food.

Cause 2: Chlorophyll takes in the Sun's energy.

Cause 3: Most plants need water to grow.

Cause 4: A plant absorbs water and carbon dioxide.

2. What does the word *absorb* mean?
   a. to set free **b.** to take in **c.** to change **d.** to become larger

3. What is *chlorophyll*, and what does it do? ____________________

____

Name: ______________________________

Photosynthesis

Directions: Think about how plants grow. Use the pictures below to help you describe the process of photosynthesis.

First, ______________________________

At the same time, ______________________________

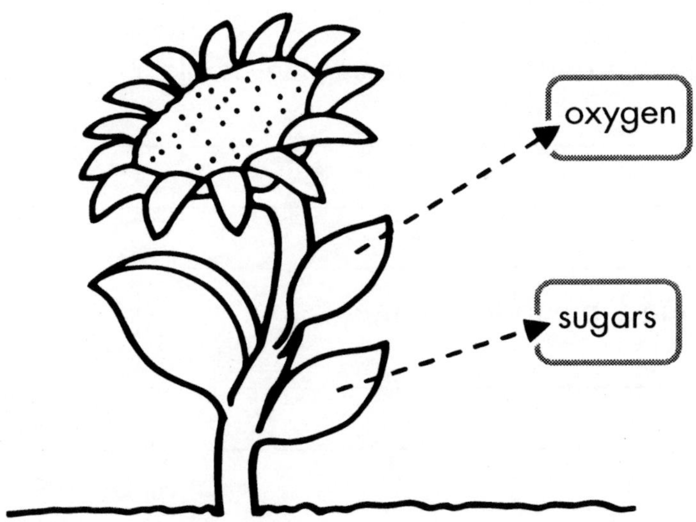

Finally, ______________________________

Name: ____

Anatomy of a Plant

I was really excited for today's garden field trip! Our plants have grown so much since we first planted our seeds. Today, Miss Walton has promised to teach us the different parts of plants. Miss Walton is my absolute favorite teacher. She always lets us do hands-on projects! When we arrived at the garden, Miss Walton immediately launched into her lecture.

"Let's look at the **roots**, **leaves**, and **stems** of our plants," said Miss Walton. "Everyone, point to a leaf on your plant. Who can tell me about how the leaves of a plant help the plant survive and grow?"

"I can!" Andy volunteered eagerly. "In order to survive and grow, plants need food. Leaves help make food for the plant through the process of photosynthesis."

"Wonderful job, Andy," Miss Walton said. "Okay, now everyone point to your plant's stems. Can someone answer the same question about stems?"

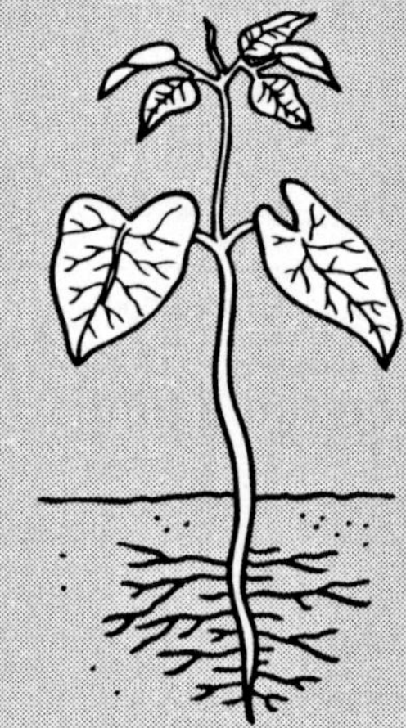

"Plants need water to survive and grow, too! The stem moves water from the plant's roots to the rest of the plant," said Emily.

I really wanted to answer one of Miss Walton's questions. I told myself I would definitely answer the next one.

"One last question—what are the roots of a plant responsible for?"

I raised my hand. "The roots absorb minerals and water from the ground. They also help keep plants stable."

"Fantastic work," Miss Walton happily replied.

1. Which of the following is *not* true about the parts of a plant? Circle your answer.
   - **a.** Each part of the plant helps it survive and grow.
   - **b.** The stem is the main part of the plant that absorbs the Sun's energy.
   - **c.** Roots absorb minerals and water from the soil.
   - **d.** Leaves are an important part of the photosynthesis process.

2. What did Miss Walton mean when she said that roots "help keep a plant stable"?

____

____

____

3. In your opinion, which part of the plant is most important? Why?

____

____

____

Name: ______________________________

Word Study—What a Plant Needs to Grow

Directions: Study the definitions. Then, use each vocabulary word in a sentence that relates to the information from this unit.

chlorophyll—the green substance in plants that makes it possible for them to make food from carbon dioxide and water

____

____

____

leaves—green and flat parts of the plant that grow from stems; makes food for the plant through the process of photosynthesis

____

____

____

photosynthesis—the process by which a green plant turns water and carbon dioxide into food when the plant is exposed to light

____

____

____

roots—the part of a plant that grows underground, gets water and minerals from the ground, and holds the plant in place

____

____

____

stems—the main long and thin part of a plant that rises above the soil and supports the leaves and flowers; moves water from the plant's roots to the rest of the plant

____

____

____

Name: ______________________________

The Structure of a Plant

Directions: Think about the different parts of a plant. Study the diagram below. Then, respond to the prompt below.

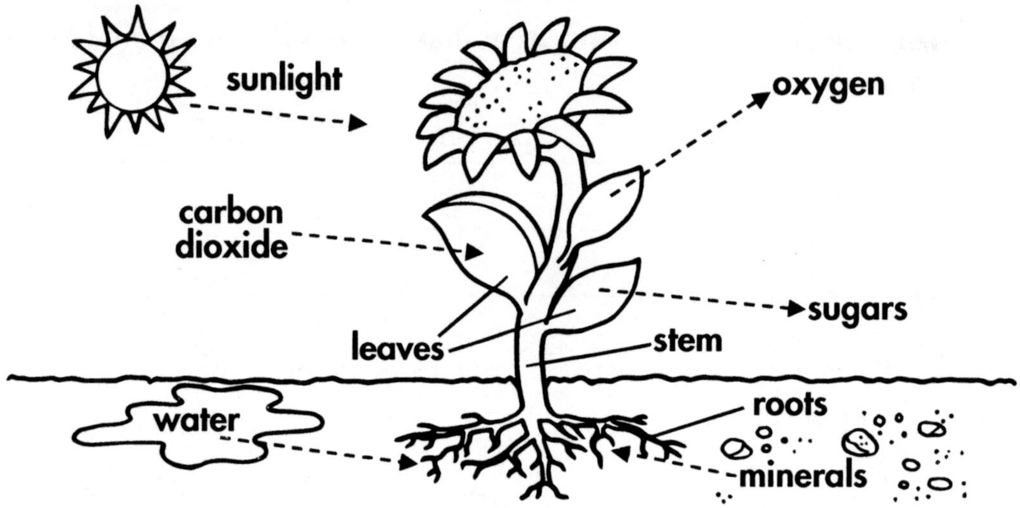

Prompt How does a plant's structure help it grow and survive?

Name: ______________________________

Let's Rock and Roll!

All rocks are pretty much the same, right? Wrong! Rocks come in all shapes, sizes, colors, and textures. But, every rock can be **classified** as one of three types. The rock types are **igneous, metamorphic**, and **sedimentary**. Each of these rock types gets its name from how it is formed.

Igneous Rocks

Igneous rock is formed from liquid rock called *magma.* This liquid rock is created beneath Earth's crust, where is it is extremely hot. When magma comes to the surface, it cools and becomes solid. This cooled magma is igneous rock.

Basalt (igneous)

Breccia (sedimentary)

Sedimentary Rocks

Over time, wind, water, and other forces wear down rock. When rocks are worn down, tiny rock pieces are transported and deposited elsewhere. These pieces of rock are called *sediment.* This sediment builds up, layer by layer. After enough time passes, the layers of sediment combine and harden to become sedimentary rock.

Metamorphic Rocks

Metamorphic rocks are rocks that have gone through a huge change. This change is usually caused by extreme pressure or heat. Both igneous and sedimentary rocks can be changed into metamorphic rocks.

Gneiss (metamorphic)

1. To *classify* is to ______________________.
   - **a.** make something by putting together parts or materials
   - **b.** arrange into groups based on ways that they are alike
   - **c.** change from a solid to a liquid because of heat

2. Draw a line to match each rock type to the correct description.

igneous	**a.** formed when sediment layers combine and harden
sedimentary	**b.** formed when magma cools and becomes hard
metamorphic	**c.** formed because of extreme pressure or heat

3. *Igneous, metamorphic,* and *sedimentary* rocks got their names because of how they were
   a. worn away. **b.** melted. **c.** formed. **d.** transferred.

4. Describe how sedimentary rock is formed.

____

____

Name: ______________________________

Three Kinds of Rocks

There are three types of rocks. They are *igneous*, *metamorphic*, and *sedimentary*. Each rock type gets its name from how it was formed.

Directions: Use the facts below to help you write paragraphs about each type of rock.

- ❍ Igneous rock is the rock type that makes up most of Earth's crust.
- ❍ Sedimentary rocks are created very slowly. They are made after sediment layers combine and harden.
- ❍ The word *metamorphic* is related to the word *metamorphosis*. This means a change in physical form, structure, or substance.
- ❍ Granite, obsidian, and basalt are all examples of igneous rock.
- ❍ Limestone is a type of sedimentary rock that is often formed from shells.
- ❍ The word *igneous* means relating to or looking like fire.
- ❍ Extreme pressure can cause igneous or sedimentary rock to change into metamorphic rock.
- ❍ Igneous rock begins as magma, which is hot, liquid rock.
- ❍ Extreme heat can cause igneous or sedimentary rock to change into metamorphic rock.
- ❍ Slate and marble are types of metamorphic rock.
- ❍ Sandstone is a type of sedimentary rock. It is usually formed by tiny grains of sand.
- ❍ Rocks wear down and are deposited elsewhere. This creates sediment.

Igneous Rock ______________________________

____

____

____

Metamorphic Rock ______________________________

____

____

____

Sedimentary Rock ______________________________

____

____

____

Name: ______________________________

Reading the Rocks

Our world is filled with amazing **landforms**. These are Earth's natural features—like mountains, plains, and glaciers. One of the most stunning landforms is found in Arizona. It is called the Grand Canyon. The Grand Canyon stretches across the northern part of the state. It is hundreds of miles long! At its deepest, the **canyon** plunges for over a mile. Though famous for its size, the true wonder of the canyon is the story its rocks tell.

We can learn a lot about the Grand Canyon by looking at its **rock layers**. These layers tell us about ancient landforms and bodies of water. They reveal the history of our Earth!

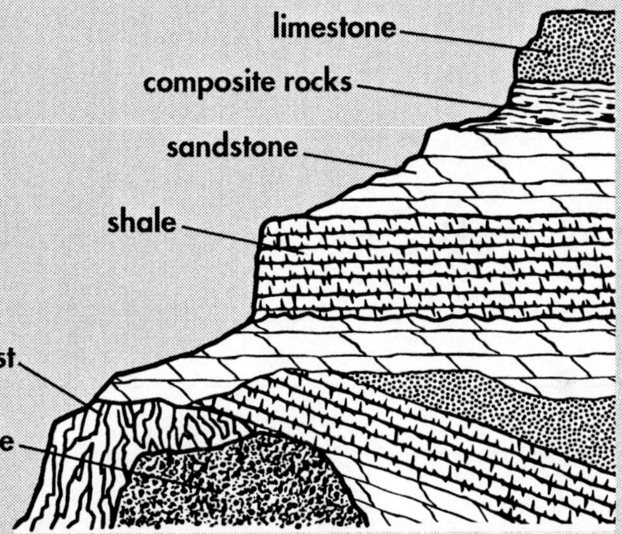

Some of the rocks at the bottom of the Grand Canyon are billions of years old! Many of these ancient rocks are granite. Granite is an igneous rock. Others are schist, which is a metamorphic rock.

On top of this rock layer are shale and sandstone. This is a type of sedimentary rock. These rocks are younger, but still very old. Throughout the canyon, there are layers of different types of sedimentary rocks. There are sandstone layers and shale layers. There are also layers of limestone.

1. Which of the following is *not* true about landforms?
   - **a.** Landforms are natural features of Earth.
   - **b.** Mountains and plains are examples of landforms.
   - **c.** Most landforms are billions of years old.
   - **d.** The Grand Canyon is a landform.

2. Based on the image above, what can you assume about the Grand Canyon?
   - **a.** Sedimentary rocks are not commonly found in the Grand Canyon.
   - **b.** The Grand Canyon has more shale than most landforms.
   - **c.** The Colorado River has been around for billions of years.
   - **d.** The Grand Canyon is made up of many different rock layers.

3. Use complete sentences to describe the Grand Canyon and its rock layers.

____

____

____

Name: ____

Word Study—Rock Types

Directions: Study the definitions. Then, use each vocabulary word in a sentence that relates to the information from this unit.

classify—to arrange things into groups based on ways that they are alike

____

____

____

igneous rock—a type of rock formed when hot, liquid rock cools and becomes hard

____

____

____

landform—a natural feature on Earth's surface

____

____

____

metamorphic rock— a type of rock that has changed forms due to the influence of heat, pressure, or other force

____

____

____

sedimentary rock—a type of rock formed when layers of sediment are deposited over time by water or air

____

____

____

Name: ____

Rock Comics

Directions: Use the following panels in order to create a comic strip about the adventures of a **geologist**—a scientist who studies rocks. Make sure to include facts about rocks in your comic strip.

If your comic strip is not finished, write *"to be continued"* in the last panel.

Comic Title:

Name: ______________________________________

Forces of Nature

Nature works in powerful ways. Over time, nature can break down or build landforms. Nature can create mountains. It can carve canyons and build sand dunes. Nature does this through certain processes called **weathering** and **erosion**.

- *Weathering* is what happens when rocks are worn down. This wearing down is caused by wind, water, and heat. Even plants and animals can cause weathering.
- *Erosion* is what happens when rock **fragments** (pieces) are carried to a new place.

Weathering and erosion often work together. A mountain is worn down by weathering. This creates rock fragments. These fragments are carried away by erosion.

1. This passage is mainly about ________________.
   - **a.** natural processes that shape Earth
   - **b.** one type of weathering that wears Earth down
   - **c.** landforms like mountains, sand dunes, and canyons
   - **d.** the different ways erosion transforms our environment
2. ______________________________ happens when rocks are worn down by forces such as wind, water, and heat.
3. Can *weathering* create new landforms? Why, or why not?

____

____

____

____

____

____

Name: ______________________________

Three Types of Weathering

Physical Weathering

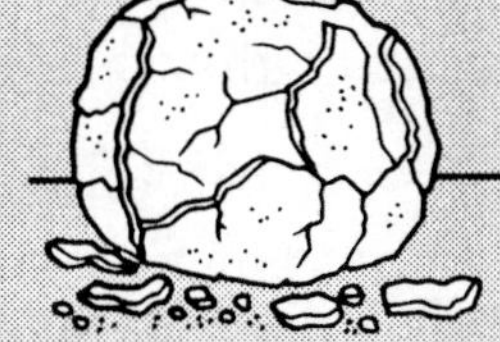

- happens when wind and water smooth or wear away rock
  Example: Over time, the wind wears down the surface of rocks.
- happens when changes in temperature make rocks expand, shrink, and break apart
  Example: Sometimes, cracks in rocks fill with water. The water turns to ice and expands. This causes pressure on the rocks. In time, the pressure will break the rocks apart.

Chemical Weathering

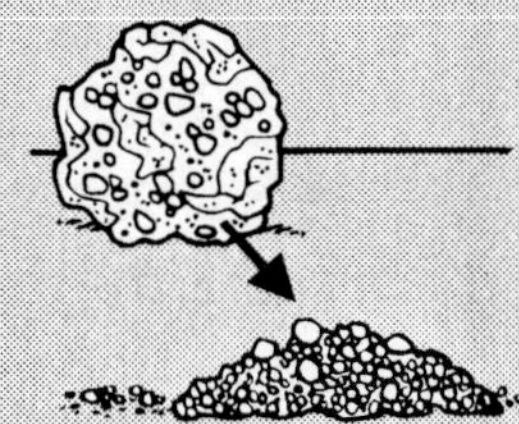

- is often caused by water
  Example: There is carbon dioxide in the air. It is created by plants, animals, and people. Carbon dioxide and pollutants dissolve in rainwater. This makes the water **acidic**. When the acidic rainwater hits rocks, it breaks them down over time.
- changes the minerals found in rocks
  Example: When iron found in rocks is exposed to water and oxygen, it can turn to rust.

Biological Weathering

- is caused by living things
  Example: Tree roots grow and break rocks apart.
  Example: Moles tunnel underground and break rocks apart.
  Example: Herds of large mammals trample over rocks and break them.

1. How is *biological weathering* different from *physical weathering*?

____

____

____

2. How are all three types of weathering similar?

____

____

____

3. Describe one example of weathering you have seen. What type of weathering was it?

____

____

____

Name: ______________________________

Carried Away

Have you ever been to a river or a beach? Have you ever seen a **landslide**? If you answered *yes* to either question, you have seen **erosion** at work.

There are examples of erosion everywhere. Like weathering, erosion is a natural process that shapes Earth. Erosion can happen in many ways:

- Rivers cause erosion. When a river moves, it wears down rocks. It then carries these rocks downstream. Over time, a river can do a lot of damage. It can even create canyons!
- Gravity can also lead to erosion. During a landslide, rocks and soil fall down hills and mountains. This is an example of erosion because the rocks and soil have been carried from one place to another.
- Waves can also cause erosion. Weathering occurs when waves crash against beaches and break down rocks. But when the waves *carry away* the rocks, this is an example of erosion.

The White Cliffs of Dover in England are slowly erroding at a rate of nearly half an inch each year.

1. Rock fragments are transported to a new place by the process of ____________________.
2. Which of the following is *not* an example of erosion?
   a. rocks and soil falling down a hill
   b. water and wind wearing down rocks over time
   c. waves carrying away rock fragments
   d. a river carrying rocks downstream
3. Describe the different ways erosion shapes land.

____

____

____

____

____

____

Name: ______________________________

Word Study—Weathering and Erosion

Directions: Study the definitions. Then, use each vocabulary word in a sentence that relates to the information from this unit.

acidic—containing acid

____

____

____

erosion—happens when rock fragments are carried away *after* being worn down

____

____

____

fragments—broken parts or pieces of something

____

____

____

landslide—a large mass of rocks and earth that suddenly and quickly moves down the side of a mountain or hill

____

____

____

weathering—happens when rocks are worn down by wind, water, temperature, plants, or animals

____

____

____

Name: ____________________________________

Weathering vs. Erosion

Directions: Think about weathering and erosion. How are they different? How are they similar? Add facts to each section of the Venn diagram.

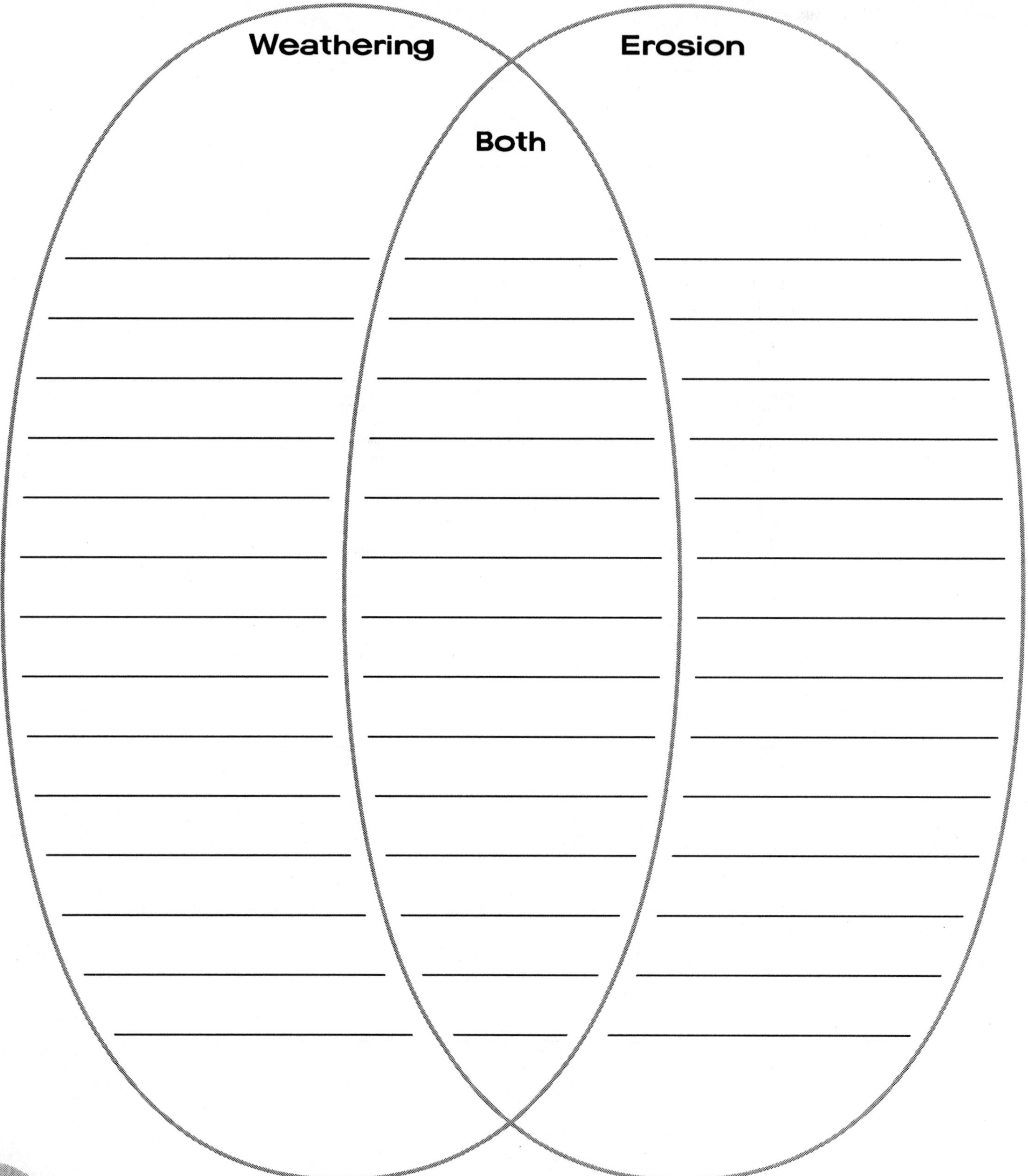

Name: ______________________________

Blast from the Past

Picture yourself at a museum. You stare in awe at the skeleton of a dinosaur. It towers above you. How did this giant skeleton make its way into the museum? The answer is simple. There are scientists who study plants and creatures that lived a long time ago. They are called **paleontologists**.

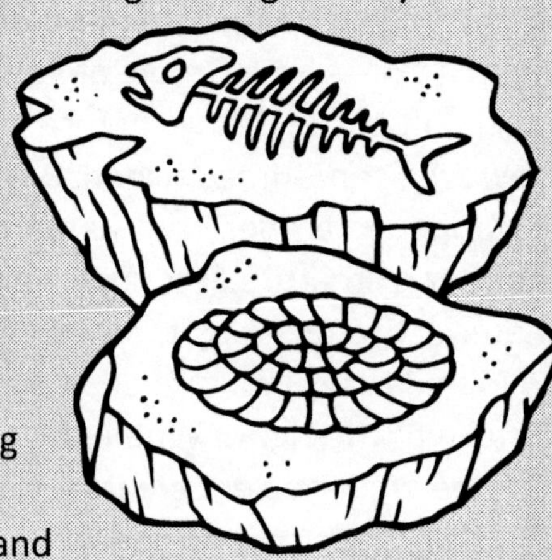

These scientists search for **fossils**, which are physical records of **ancient** life. Fossils can include the **remains** of plants and creatures from millions of years ago. They can also include **traces** of life. It might be a rock that shows the shape of a leaf—or it could be the footprint of an ancient creature.

Fossils are usually created when the remains of a living thing sink underwater. In most cases, this is something hard, such as the bones of a fish. As time passes, layers of rocks and soil cover the remains. Then, these layers become solid and are changed into rocks. In this way, remains of the living thing are preserved, waiting to be discovered!

1. Which of the following is an example of a *fossil*?
   - **a.** a sunken ship from hundreds of years ago
   - **b.** the ruins of a medieval castle
   - **c.** a crumpled leaf, floating in a stream
   - **d.** the footprint of a dinosaur preserved in stone
2. The *remains* and *traces* of ancient living things are called ______________________.
3. Use complete sentences to describe how *fossils* are created.

____

____

____

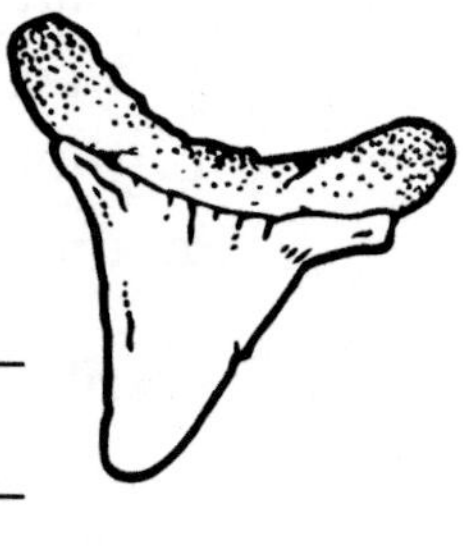

____

____

____

____

____

Name: ____

A Fantastic Find

In 2015, scientists made a great find. They found the tail of a dinosaur trapped in **amber**. The tail was 99 million years old! This find was unlike any that had been made before.

In most cases, fossils are not created from **soft tissue**. Animal skin is an example of soft tissue. That is because most soft tissue **decays** before it can be preserved. However, sometimes scientists are lucky, and soft tissue is trapped in amber. This happens when the remains of a plant or a creature gets covered in **resin**. Resin is a sticky material produced by trees. Over time, resin becomes solid and turns into amber. Notice the ant in resin in the picture to the right. When life is preserved in amber, we can see what ancient creatures really looked like.

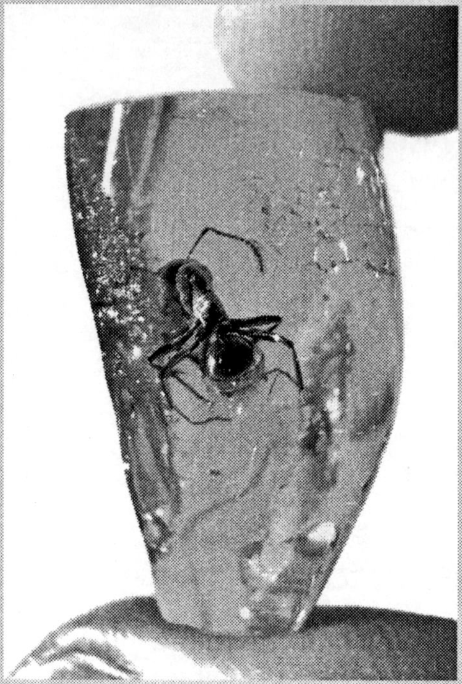

Ant trapped in amber

So, what did the dinosaur tail found in amber tell us? It proved that dinosaurs had feathers! Scientists have long believed in feathered dinosaurs. There are dinosaur fossils that show traces of feathers. However, this tail was the strongest proof of feathered dinosaurs that had ever been found. It showed actual feathers attached to a dinosaur tail!

1. Why are fossils containing *soft tissue* rare?
   - **a.** most amber fossils trap hard materials such as bone and shells
   - **b.** most soft tissue decays before it can be fossilized
   - **c.** fossils containing soft tissue are not rare
   - **d.** prehistoric creatures did not have much soft tissue

2. What did scientists learn from the fossilized dinosaur tail?
   - **a.** that over time, resin turns into amber
   - **b.** that dinosaurs lived millions of years ago
   - **c.** that soft tissue can be trapped in amber
   - **d.** that there were feathered dinosaurs

3. Describe the process that created the fossilized dinosaur tail.

____

____

____

____

Name: ______________________________

Word Study—Fossils

Directions: Study the definitions. Then, use each vocabulary word in a sentence that relates to the information from this unit.

ancient—very old; having lived or existed for a very long time

____

____

____

decay—to be slowly broken down by the natural processes that destroy a dead plant or body

____

____

____

fossil—the traces or remains of a plant or animal that lived in ancient times and that you can see in some rocks

____

____

____

paleontologist—a scientist who studies the fossils of animals and plants that lived very long ago, especially in the time of dinosaurs

____

____

____

remains—the dead body of a person or animal

____

____

____

resin—a yellow or brown sticky substance that comes from some trees

____

____

____

Name: ______________________________

Featuring Fossils

Directions: Imagine you are a news reporter. You are writing an article about fossils. Your article should include examples of fossils and how they are created. Remember to write a headline for your article and a caption for the photo.

The Fossil Record

Writer: ______________________________ **Date:** ______________

____

(headline)

Caption: ______________________________

Name: ______________________________

Journey Through Earth

It's almost time. You will go where no human has gone before. You are journeying to the center of Earth!

First, you travel through Earth's outermost layer, the **crust**. Earth's crust is its thinnest layer. It is the layer that is made up of **tectonic plates**, giant moving masses of rock. This part of the journey goes quickly because the crust is less than 30 miles deep.

After you move past the crust, the temperature rises. You have made it to the **mantle**. Traveling through the mantle will be the longest part of your journey. The mantle is Earth's thickest layer. It is 1,800 miles thick.

Scientists think of the mantle in two parts: the upper mantle and the lower mantle. The upper mantle is closer to the crust and is completely solid. The lower mantle is a mixture of solid and liquid rock called **magma**. The farther you move through the mantle, the hotter it gets.

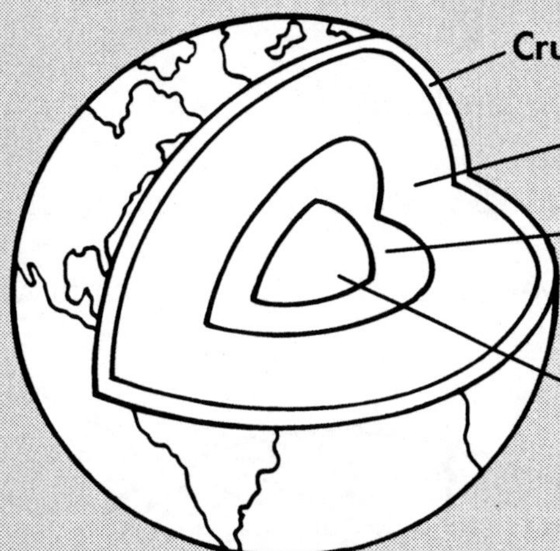

Next, you reach Earth's **outer core**. This layer is liquid and very, very hot. This layer of Earth is formed of nickel and iron.

Finally, you reach Earth's **inner core**! This is the hottest layer of Earth. Even though it is extremely hot, the core is solid, not liquid. The core is solid because of the pressure created by the other layers of Earth. Earth's solid center is formed mostly of iron.

You did it! You traveled to the center of Earth. Now, it's time to return to the surface!

1. From outermost layer to innermost layer, these are the four layers of Earth:

____

____

2. Study the image above. What are two observations you can make about Earth and its layers based on the image?

____

____

____

____

Name: ______________________________

Earth's Layers

Directions: Think about what you have learned about Earth's layers. Match each sentence starter with its correct ending.

_______ **1.** The thinnest layer of Earth is

_______ **2.** The solid, hot center of Earth is

_______ **3.** Surrounding the inner core is the liquid

_______ **4.** The widest layer of Earth is

_______ **5.** The crust is made up of

(a) moving rock masses.

(b) the mantle.

(c) the inner core.

(d) the crust.

(e) outer core.

Label It! Label the layers of Earth on the image below.

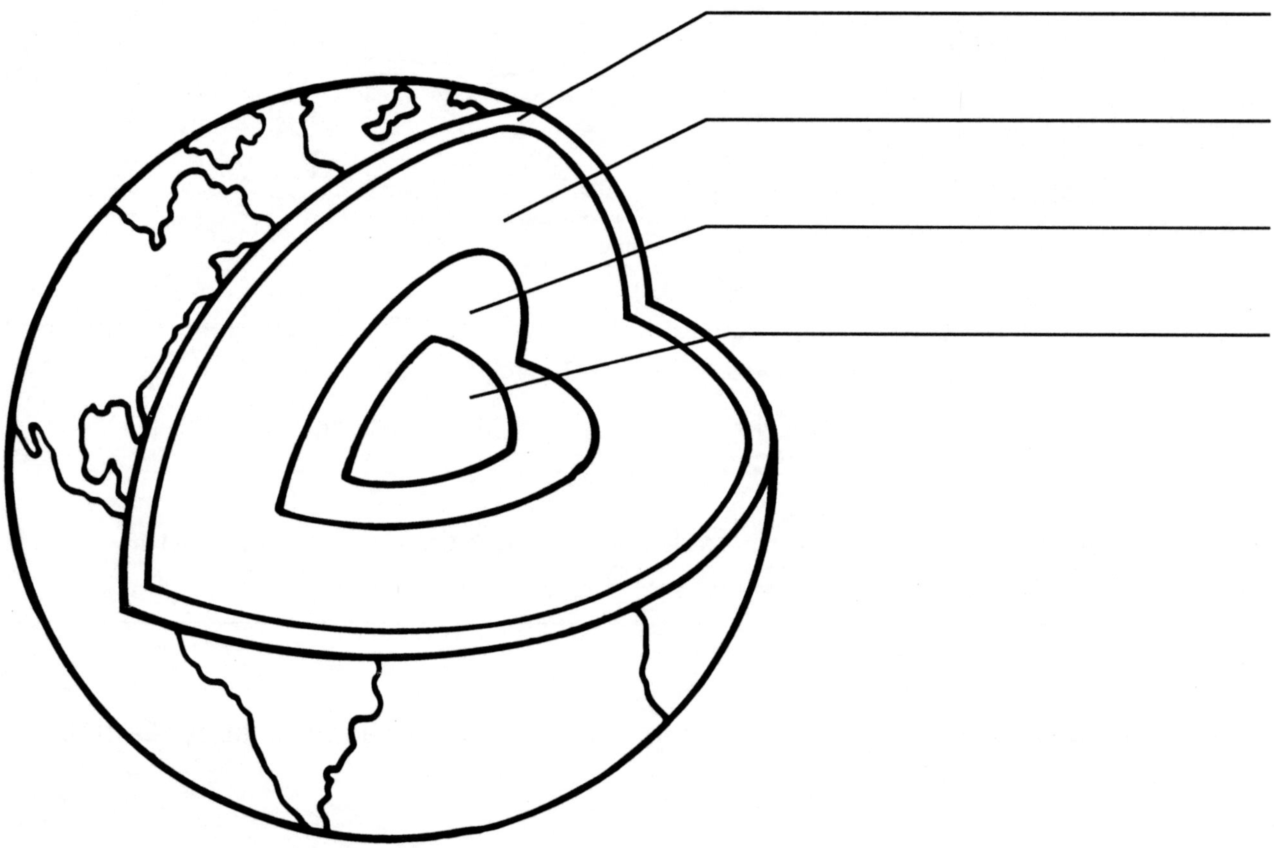

1. Which layer is made up of tectonic plates? ______________________________

2. List Earth's layers from hottest to coldest:

____

____

Name: ____

Word Study—Layers of Earth

Directions: Study the definitions. Then, use each vocabulary word in a sentence that relates to the information from this unit.

crust—the outermost and thinnest layer of Earth, made up of moving masses of rock called tectonic plates

____

____

____

inner core—the hottest layer of Earth, made mostly of iron and completely solid

____

____

____

magma—the melted rock that makes up the mantle

____

____

____

mantle—the widest layer of Earth, made up of the upper mantle (solid) and lower mantle (solid and liquid)

____

____

____

outer core—the hot, liquid layer of Earth that surrounds the inner core and is made of nickel and iron

____

____

____

Name: ______________________________

My Great Journey

Directions: Use the following panels to create a comic strip or a story about your journey to Earth's center. Make sure to include facts about the layers of Earth.

If your comic strip is not finished, write *"to be continued"* in the last panel.

Name: ______________________________

Kaboom!

Krakatoa is a famous volcano. It once blocked out the Sun. For many years, the volcano was **dormant**. This means that it was not active. But in 1883, that changed. The volcano had a series of huge **eruptions**.

Krakatoa erupting in 2008

After its long period of being dormant, Krakatoa erupted four times. The volcano sent great amounts of ash into the air. This ash blocked out the Sun for days. The explosions were loud. They were heard thousands of miles away!

Even though people did not live on the island, thousands were killed during the explosion. The eruptions were very powerful. They caused giant waves that destroyed many villages on nearby islands.

Krakatoa is found in a dangerous part of the world. It lies on the **boundary** between two **tectonic plates**. These are moving rock masses. They make up Earth's outer layer. Plate boundaries are dangerous places. When two plates collide or move past each other, they can cause disaster. The movement of these plates can cause earthquakes and volcanic eruptions.

1. A volcano that is not active is called a ______________________ volcano.
2. What makes the island of Krakatoa likely to erupt? Circle your answer.
   - **a.** its great size
   - **b.** the amount of ash it sent into the air
   - **c.** its location on a plate boundary
   - **d.** its period of being dormant
3. Do you think Krakatoa deserves to be famous? Why, or why not?

Name: ____

Word Study—Volcanoes

Directions: Study the definitions. Then, use each vocabulary word in a sentence that relates to the information from this unit.

boundary—something (such as a river, a fence, or an imaginary line) that shows where an area ends and another area begins

____

____

____

dormant—not active but able to become active

____

____

____

eruption—sending out rocks, ash, and lava in a sudden explosion

____

____

____

tectonic plates—moving rock masses that make up Earth's outer layer

____

____

____

volcano—a mountain or hill with a crater or vent(s) on the top or side that sometimes sends out rocks, ash, gases, and lava in an eruption

____

____

____

Name: ____________________

Parts of a Volcano

Volcanoes shape our world. When volcanoes erupt, they spew **rocks**, **lava**, and **ash**. Over many years, the rocks, ash, and lava build up, layer by layer. In time, landforms such as islands and mountains are created. The Hawaiian Islands were formed in this way.

Deep within Earth, there is **magma**. This is melted rock. During an eruption, magma moves through **vents** in a volcano. Some volcanoes have more than one vent. The main vent leads to the **crater**, which is a large bowl-like opening in a volcano. A crater is formed when the top of a mountain explodes after an eruption! When magma reaches a vent, rocks, lava, and ash spew from the volcano.

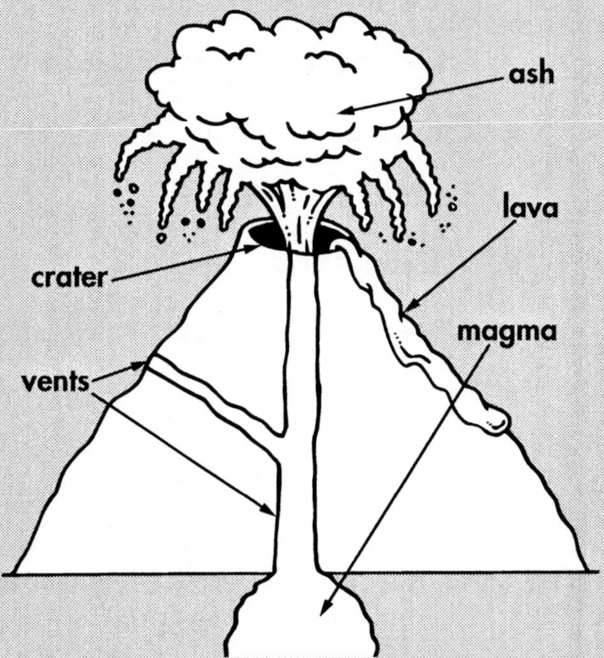

In summary, erupting volcanoes have different parts:

crater: the bowl-like opening of a volcano

vent: an opening in a volcano where magma can escape

magma: melted rock within Earth

lava: melted rock that comes out of a volcano

ash: bits of magma that have exploded into the air

1. When magma escapes from a vent, it comes out as rocks, ____________________ and ____________________.

2. How do volcanoes create landforms? Circle your answer.
   - **a.** Eruptions of ash and lava build up over time.
   - **b.** Islands become smaller due to melted rock and ash.
   - **c.** Magma is found deep underground as melted rock.
   - **d.** Most landforms on Earth used to be volcanoes.

3. Describe what happens when a volcano erupts. Be sure to include the parts of a volcano in your description.

____

____

____

____

Name: ____________________________________

Understanding Volcanoes

Directions: Think about what you have learned about volcanoes. Match each sentence starter with its correct ending.

_______ **1.** The bowl-like opening in a volcano is called

_______ **2.** Eruptions are more likely to happen on the boundaries of

_______ **3.** Many volcanoes are inactive, or

_______ **4.** Ash is created when

_______ **5.** Melted rock called

_______ **6.** Volcanoes create landforms like

_______ **7.** When magma flows from a volcano, it is called

_______ **8.** When lava, rocks, and ash spew from a volcano, it is called

(a) islands and mountains.

(b) a crater.

(c) lava.

(d) an eruption.

(e) tectonic plates.

(f) magma moves through volcanic vents.

(g) bits of magma explode into the air.

(h) dormant.

Label It! Label the volcano below using words from the Word Bank.

Word Bank

ash
crater
lava
magma
main vent
side vent

Name: ______________________________

On Krakatoa

Directions: Imagine you are on the island when Krakatoa erupts. What do you see? What do you do? Write a journal entry of your experience below.

Name: ______________________________

Terrible Temblors

It's just a regular afternoon. You are lounging on the couch watching TV. In the middle of your favorite program, the room begins to shake. A bookcase falls over. The television rattles off the table and crashes to the ground. You are in the middle of a **temblor**!

Temblors are what scientists call earthquakes. They happen all the time. We don't feel most earthquakes, but when we do, they can be very scary. At least one large earthquake happens each year.

Earthquakes are caused when large rock masses shift below the surface of Earth. These rock masses are called **tectonic plates**. They make up Earth's outer layer, which is called the **crust**.

When tectonic plates collide or grind against each other, pressure builds. Eventually, this pressure becomes too much, and plates move abruptly along a **fault**. A fault is a fracture or crack in Earth's crust.

When tectonic plates move along a fault, this creates **seismic waves**. These waves of energy move through Earth and across its surface. When seismic waves are strong, the ground shakes and shifts, creating an earthquake.

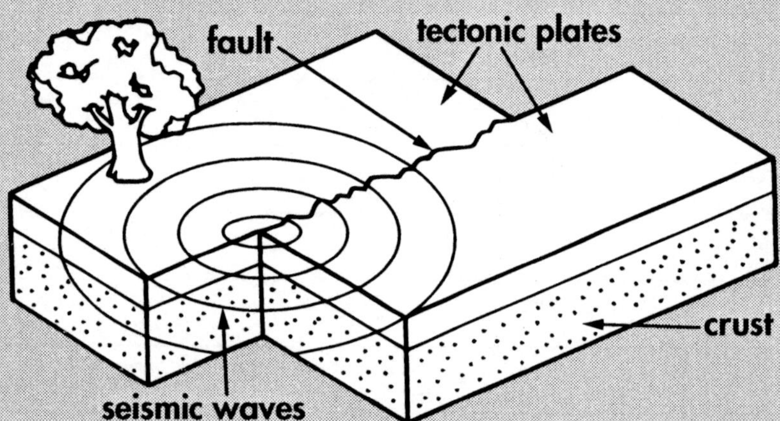

1. Earthquakes are caused by the movement of ______________________________ found below Earth's surface.

2. When tectonic plates move suddenly along a ____________________, seismic waves of energy move through Earth and across its surface.

3. Think about what causes an earthquake. Put the steps in order from 1–5. The first one has been done for you.

   ______ This movement causes pressure to build between the two plates.

   ______ Then, seismic waves move through Earth.

   __1__ Two tectonic plates move against each other.

   ______ These waves of energy cause the ground to shift and shake.

   ______ Once the pressure is too much, the plates move suddenly along a fault.

Name: ______________________________

Word Study—Earthquakes

Directions: Study the definitions. Then, use each vocabulary word in a sentence that relates to the information from this unit.

convergent—moving toward; approaching

____

____

divergent—moving away from

____

____

fault—a break or crack in Earth's crust

____

____

____

seismic waves—waves of energy caused by an earthquake

____

____

____

subducts—when the edge of one tectonic plate moves under the edge of another

____

____

temblor—an earthquake

____

____

____

Name: ______________________________

Three Types of Plate Boundaries

Tectonic plates are moving rock masses. They make up Earth's crust. Tectonic plates are often described by their boundaries. There are three types of plate boundaries:

A ***convergent*** **plate boundary** happens when two plates *move toward* each other. Part of one plate **subducts**, or goes under, the other plate. This part of the plate is destroyed. → ←

A ***divergent*** **plate boundary** occurs when two plates *move away* from each other. New crust is created from rising magma. This crust moves into the place where the two plates separated. ← →

A ***transform*** **plate boundary** happens when two plates *slide alongside* each other. These plates often cause earthquakes. ⇄

Directions: Study the images. Then, complete the sentences with *convergent*, *divergent*, or *transform*. Each word should only be used once.

1.

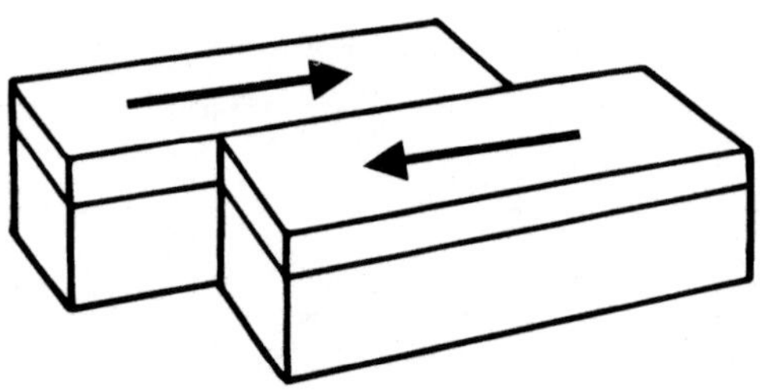

Tectonic plates slide past each other in a ______________________________ plate boundary.

2.

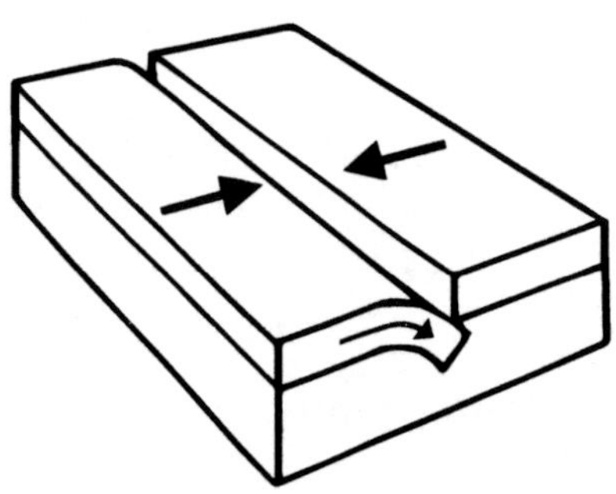

One plate subducts under another plate in a ______________________________ plate boundary.

3.

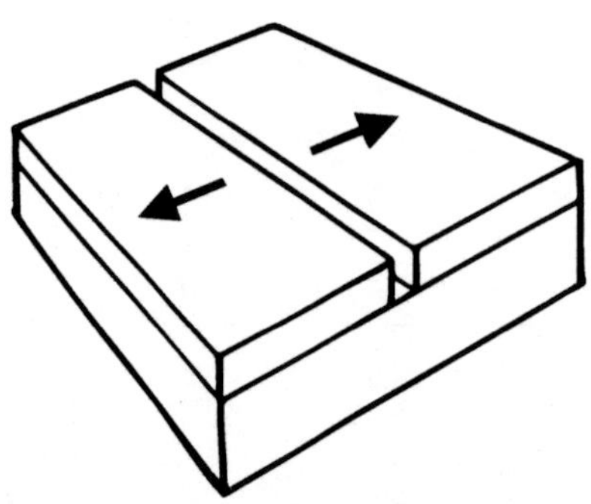

New crust is created as two plates move apart in a ________________________ plate boundary.

Name: ______________________________

Writing About Earthquakes

Directions: Think about earthquakes and tectonic plates. Use the Word Bank to help you answer the questions below.

Word Bank

- convergent plate boundary
- crust
- divergent plate boundary
- fault
- seismic waves
- subducts
- temblor
- transform plate boundary

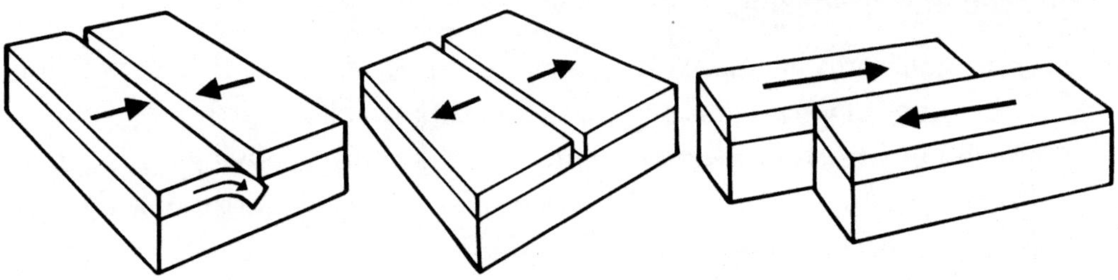

1. What are tectonic plates? ______________________________

____

____

2. How do tectonic plates interact with each other? ______________________________

____

____

____

3. How do tectonic plates cause earthquakes? ______________________________

____

____

____

Name: ______________________________

Ready for Anything

Earthquakes can happen at any time. The best way to stay safe is to be prepared. When it comes to quakes, it's important to be ready for anything.

One of the best ways to prepare is to make your home more earthquake safe. Next time you are home, walk through each room. Do you see any potential **hazards**—things that may be sources of danger? Look at the heavy items, such as TVs, large mirrors, or bookcases. Can they be firmly attached, or **secured,** to a wall so that they do not fall on anyone?

There are different ways to make sure items are secure. Large items may be secured with closed hooks or flexible straps. These straps let objects move with earthquakes but keep them from falling to the ground. Cabinet doors should have strong latches that will stay closed during shaking.

Even small items like books and lamps can become hazards if sent flying. These can be secured in a number of ways. You might use something called earthquake putty. This is a sticky material that can be attached to objects and keep them from moving during an earthquake. If you do all of the above, your home will be much safer during an earthquake. Can you think of other things you might do to make your home safer?

1. Heavy items such as bookcases need to be firmly attached, or ______________________.
2. Open cabinets can be potential ______________________ because items may fall from shelves during an earthquake.
3. Which of the following is a potential earthquake hazard? Circle your answer.
   - **a.** a large rug underneath a sofa
   - **b.** a mirror that is not securely attached to a wall
   - **c.** a lamp attached to a table with earthquake putty
   - **d.** cabinet doors with strong latches
4. Think about items in your home. Which items are potential hazards during an earthquake?

   ____

   How could you make them safer? ______________________________

   ____

   ____

Name: ______________________________

Superior Structures

Earthquakes are very powerful. They can even be deadly. In the past, strong earthquakes have destroyed entire cities. But, there are ways to reduce an earthquake's **impact**, or effects. One of the best ways to do so is to build structures that are made to withstand earthquakes.

Today, when engineers design large buildings, they think about how it will be impacted by a great earthquake. They have learned that there are certain things that make large buildings more earthquake resistant. Buildings that have strong **foundations** are more likely to stay standing during a quake. These foundations are structures made of stone or cement. They provide support *under* a building.

We often think of buildings as solid structures that do not move—but when an earthquake hits, it pushes against buildings. If a building is not **flexible**, it can crumble. Some of today's tallest skyscrapers are built to be flexible. They move from side to side when an earthquake strikes.

The Shanghai Tower was designed to be earthquake resistant.

1. This text is mainly about ____________________.
   - **a.** how earthquakes are caused and how they move
   - **b.** how engineers design buildings with earthquakes in mind
   - **c.** how flexibility is important in very tall buildings
   - **d.** how strong foundations reduce a quake's impact on a building

2. How do engineers design buildings to be more earthquake-proof?
   - **a.** They design buildings that do not move, no matter how powerful the quake.
   - **b.** They design strong foundations that provide support underneath buildings.
   - **c.** They make sure buildings are flexible and able to sway with an earthquake's tremors.
   - **d.** both **b** and **c**

3. Describe a building that would not be safe during an earthquake.

____

____

____

____

Name: ______________________________

Word Study—Preparing for Earthquakes

Directions: Study the definitions. Then, use each vocabulary word in a sentence that relates to the information from this unit.

flexible—capable of bending or being bent

____

____

____

foundations—usually stone or concrete structures that support a building from underneath

____

____

____

hazards—sources of danger

____

____

____

impact—a powerful or major influence or effect

____

____

____

secure—firmly attached

____

____

____

Name: ______________________________

Directions: Read the passage below and study the images. Then, complete the following page.

The Taipei 101 Skyscraper

This is a skyscraper in Taipei, Taiwan. Its name is Taipei 101. Taipei 101 was once the tallest building in the world. The skyscraper was designed to withstand strong winds and earthquakes. It contains something called a *tuned mass damper*.

The damper is a giant globe that weighs 728 tons—as much as 132 elephants! The globe is on the 87th floor. It is suspended by cables within the building. If this skyscraper is hit with an earthquake, the globe will sway. It will move like a pendulum, back and forth. By moving like this, the damper will decrease the building's movement, protecting the building.

Tuned mass damper

Name: ______________________________

The Taipei 101 Skyscraper *(cont.)*

Directions: Study the picture and captions. Then, answer the prompt below.

Named after its 101 stories

Designed to look like a stalk of bamboo

There are 8 sections, with 8 stories in each section. The number 8 is believed to be lucky in China.

1,667 feet tall

Prompt Would you describe the Taipei 101 as secure? Why, or why not?

____

____

____

____

____

____

____

____

____

____

____

Name: ____________________

Thinking Like an Engineer

Directions: Think about earthquake-proof buildings. Use the Word Bank to help you respond to the prompt below.

Word Bank		
cement	flexible	pendulum
damper	foundation	stone

Prompt Imagine you are an engineer. How would you design a building to be earthquake resistant?

____

Directions: Draw your building.

Name: ______________________________________

Flood Alert!

Think about where you live. Is your home in a small town or a big city? No matter where you live, there are probably buildings, cars, roads, and people. Now, imagine your town during a flood. Everything you know is underwater and likely destroyed.

This is a reality for many people. Floods happen around the world and create a lot of destruction. Floods have many different causes.

Floods can be caused by powerful storms. Floods can also be caused by underwater earthquakes. Such earthquakes cause **tsunamis**—huge, dangerous waves. Some floods are caused by a long period of rainfall. Floods can even happen when a **dam** or a **levee** breaks.

- A *dam* is a **structure** that stops the flow of water. It is usually built across a stream or a river. Some dams are **artificial**, which means they are built by humans. Others are natural dams built by animals like beavers.
- A *levee* is also a structure that stops the flow of water and prevents flooding. Levees are walls of soil that are often built along rivers. Some levees are manmade; others are created by nature.

Levees (A and B) beside a river with a small dam (C)

1. Which of the following is an example of something *artificial*?

   a. a mountain **b.** a tree **c.** a chair **d.** an animal

2. Both ________________ and ________________ are structures that stop the flow of water.

3. What are three different causes of floods?

____

____

____

____

____

Name: ______________________________

Word Study—Floods

Directions: Study the definitions. Then, use each vocabulary word in a sentence that relates to the information from this unit.

artificial—not happening or existing naturally; created or caused by people

____

____

____

dam—a structure that is built across a river or stream to stop water from flowing

____

____

____

levee—a long wall of soil built along a river to prevent flooding

____

____

____

structure—something (such as a house, a tower, or a bridge) that is built by putting parts together and that usually stands on its own

____

____

____

tsunami—a very high, large wave in the ocean that is usually caused by an underwater earthquake and that can cause great destruction when it reaches land

____

____

____

Name: ______________________________

A Safer Space

Directions: Read the passage below and study the image. Then, complete the following page.

We can't completely prevent flooding. During a heavy storm, flooding will happen, but we can make our homes safer. We can arrange our homes in a way that will help them weather the storm.

Some of the best ways to flood-proof a house are simple. If you **elevate**, or raise up, important items, you can keep them from being damaged. In the kitchen, cupboards and appliances can be raised off the floor with attachable legs. This allows water to flow through the house during a flood without damaging the kitchen units. Air-conditioning and heating units can also be elevated.

Another way to flood-proof a home is to use drains and pumps. This is helpful for homes that face flooding often. Drains are placed at low points in a house, and water is pumped outside. There are also special pumps called *sump pumps* that are placed in basements. These pumps are also used to remove water from the home. These are just a few ways to make your home a safer space during a flood!

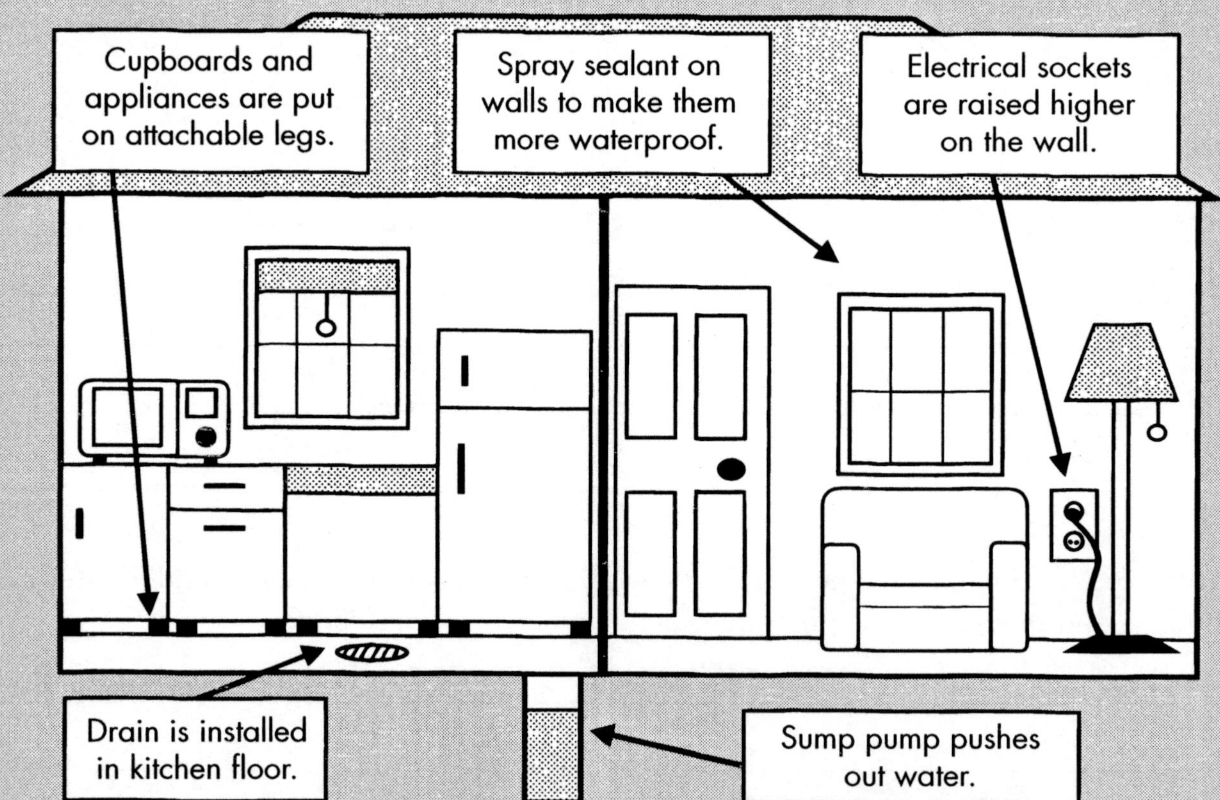

Name: ______________________________

A Safer Space *(cont.)*

1. Look at the image captions on the previous page. A *sealant* is likely a substance ________.
   - **a.** that is impossible to remove
   - **b.** that seals something, making it airtight or watertight
   - **c.** used to protect homes during all types of natural disasters
   - **d.** that is easy to remove or chip away
2. You can make your home more flood-proof if you ______________________, or raise up, important items.
3. Think about your home. What changes might be made to make your home more flood-proof?

Change 1 ______________________________

____

____

____

____

____

Change 2 ______________________________

____

____

____

____

____

Change 3 ______________________________

____

____

____

____

____

Name: ______________________________

Preparing for a Flood

Directions: Complete the sentences with the vocabulary words found in the Word Bank.

Word Bank			
artificial	elevate	prevent	sealant
dams	levee	pump	tsunamis

1. ____________________ stop water flow and are made by both people and animals.
2. Some houses install a ____________________ in the basement to help push out water during flooding.
3. There are many ways to help ____________________ damage to your home during a flood.
4. ____________________ dams are built by people. Natural dams are built by animals.
5. Monster waves, called ____________________, are often caused by underwater earthquakes.
6. Walls can be sprayed with a ____________________, making them more airtight and waterproof.
7. When preparing for a flood, it is best to ____________________ appliances above the ground.
8. A ____________________ is usually built using soil and can be an artificial or natural flood barrier.

Draw It! Draw a picture of a dam or levee in the box below. Label your drawing.

Name: ______________________________

Flood Ready

Directions: Think about the different ways to make a building more flood-proof. Use the Word Bank to help you respond to the prompt below.

Word Bank		
appliances	elevate	pump
drain	levee	sealant

Prompt Think about an important building in your life. It might be your school or home. What changes could you make to this building to make it more flood-proof?

____

____

____

____

____

____

____

____

Directions: Draw a picture of the building and the changes you would make to it.

Name: ______________________________

Earth's Resources

Imagine yourself in a forest. As you breathe in the clean air, you watch the Sun filter through the trees. You can hear the sounds of water rushing in a river close by. You are surrounded by **natural resources**.

Water, air, and sunlight are examples of natural resources. These are things made by nature that humans use to survive or improve their lives. Plants, animals, coal, and soil are also natural resources.

Not all resources are the same. Some are more easily produced by nature. These are called **renewable resources**. They include water, air, sunlight, plants, and animals.

There are also **nonrenewable resources**. These are things that are not easily created by nature. They include soil, coal, and oil. When humans use them, they can take millions of years to be replaced by nature.

Trees are renewable resources.

1. There are two types of natural resources. They are ______________________ and ______________________.

2. Coal and oil are examples of ______________________ resources because ____.

3. Plants and sunlight are examples of ______________________ resources because ____.

Name: ______________________________

Types of Resources

There are two types of natural resources. They are **renewable** and **nonrenewable**.

- *Renewable resources* are all around us. They are easy for nature to make. They include water, air, plants, and animals. The Sun shines daily and can provide light and heat. Plants grow quickly. Dairy animals, such as cows and goats, can provide us with milk.
- *Nonrenewable resources* are rarer. They take a long time to form. They can take millions of years for nature to make. Soil, oil, coal, and stone are some examples.

Renewable or Nonrenewable?

Directions: For each picture, write *renewable* if the natural resource is renewable or *nonrenewable* if the natural resource is not renewable. Then, explain how you know.

1

Crops are a ____________________

natural resource because plants __________

______________________________.

2

Light is a ____________________

natural resource because sunlight __________

______________________________.

3

Gasoline, a type of oil, is a __________

____

natural resource because oil __________

______________________________.

4

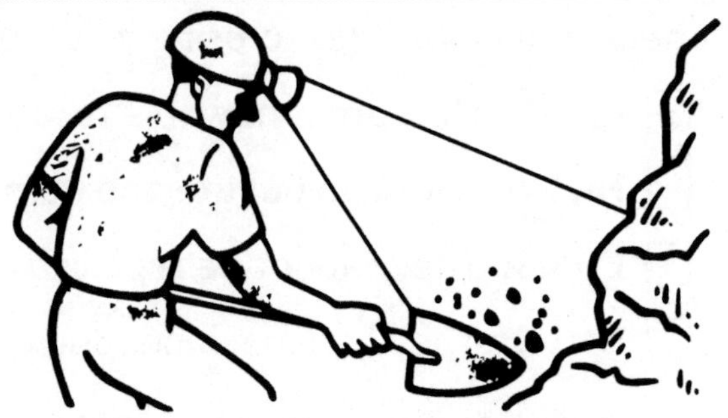

Coal, often used to make electricity, is a

____

natural resource because coal __________

______________________________.

Name: ______________________________

The Fuel of Modern Life

Powering today's world takes *a lot* of energy. We need energy to drive our cars, heat our homes, and power our machines. But where does all this energy come from?

Much of this energy comes from **fossil fuels**. These are *nonrenewable* resources. When we drive a car, ride a bus, or fly on a plane, we are using fossil fuels. Some examples of fossil fuels are coal, petroleum, and natural gas.

- We use coal to heat our homes.
- We use petroleum to make gasoline.
- Natural gas is used to light some stoves.

Fossil fuels are the ancient remains of plants and other living things. Over millions of years, these remains were covered up with layers of soil. Eventually, they were transformed into fossil fuels.

There are a few big drawbacks to using fossil fuels. One of the main drawbacks is that we use them far too quickly. Fossil fuels cannot be replaced. Fossil fuels also pollute and damage our environment. For these reasons, it is vital that we find better ways to power machines. This may include using solar or wind energy. These energy sources are renewable. They do not cause **pollution**.

1. This passage is mainly about ______________________________.

- **a.** a fossil fuel called petroleum and the way it is used
- **b.** how fossil fuels were created and how they are used
- **c.** different machines that are powered by fossil fuels
- **d.** renewable sources of energy such as solar and wind energy

2. Check two downsides to using fossil fuels.

- ☐ **Fact 1:** They are renewable resources.
- ☐ **Fact 2:** They can pollute and damage the environment.
- ☐ **Fact 3:** They cannot be replaced.
- ☐ **Fact 4:** They fuel machines such as cars and planes.

3. Use complete sentences to describe how fossil fuels were created.

____

____

____

____

Name: ______________________________

Word Study—Natural Resources

Directions: Study the definitions. Then, use each vocabulary word in a sentence that relates to the information from this unit.

fossil fuels—a fuel (such as coal, oil, or natural gas) that is formed in Earth from dead plants or animals

____

____

____

natural resource—something made by nature that humans use to survive or improve their lives

____

____

____

nonrenewable—not able to grow again or be created again; not able to be replaced by nature

____

____

____

pollution—substances that make land, water, and air dirty and not safe for use

____

____

____

renewable—restored or replaced by natural processes; able to be replaced by nature

____

____

____

Name: ______________________________

My Science Blog—Natural Resources

Directions: Imagine you are writing a blog post about natural resources. Your post should include details about *renewable* and *nonrenewable* resources. Remember to give your blog post a title.

____
(Title)

Natural resources are everywhere. Here are three examples of natural resources...

- Example 1: ______________________________
- Example 2: ______________________________
- Example 3: ______________________________

Some natural resources are renewable. This means...

Some natural resources are nonrenewable. This means...

Trees are renewable resources.

Fossil fuels are a type of nonrenewable resource. Here are three facts about fossil fuels...

- Fact 1: ______________________________
- Fact 2: ______________________________
- Fact 3: ______________________________

Name: ______________________________

The Way We Live Matters

We make thousands of choices each day. We choose what to eat and drink, where to go, and when to go. Some of these choices help the **environment**. Others cause **pollution**, dirtying our water, land, and air.

Pollution comes in many forms. It is the smog in the air. It is plastic litter at the beach. It is **toxic** chemicals, polluting our water. Pollution harms all living things. It destroys animal homes and kills wildlife. Pollution is thought to cause climate change. It may even be the source of serious illnesses such as cancer.

Pollution is caused by the choices of many people. We can help stop pollution by making different choices. Many of these choices are simple. We can stop using single-use plastic. These are items such as plastic water bottles and plastic bags. Another way to help is to **recycle** glass, paper, and plastic trash. If we do just a few small things to help the environment, we can make a big difference!

1. What does the word *toxic* likely mean?

   a. fluid **b.** clear **c.** poisonous **d.** harmless

2. Circle the two details that support the following main idea.

   Main Idea Pollution damages the environment in many ways.

   Detail 1: Pollution causes all types of illnesses.

   Detail 2: Pollution destroys animal homes and kills wildlife.

   Detail 3: Pollution damages the air and water, but not land.

   Detail 4: Pollution dirties our air, water, and land.

3. Describe three examples of *pollution*. Use complete sentences in your response.

   Example 1: ______________________________

   Example 2: ______________________________

   Example 3: ______________________________

Name: ______________________________

Types of Pollution and How to Help

Directions: Study the chart. Then, respond to the questions below.

Types of Pollution	How to Help
Water pollution includes trash found in the ocean and other bodies of water. Common examples of trash include plastic water bottles, plastic bags, and plastic straws. Animals can be harmed or killed when they mistake plastic for food. Plastic is also thought to leak deadly chemicals into the ocean.	 We can reduce water pollution by purchasing reusable bottles instead of single-use plastic bottles. We can also use cloth bags instead of plastic bags.
Air pollution includes gases such as carbon dioxide and methane. These gases contribute to climate change. Carbon dioxide is released when we drive cars, fly on planes, or power factories with fossil fuels such as coal. 	We can reduce air pollution by using cleaner sources of energy such as solar and wind energy. We can power our factories with these sources of energy instead of fossil fuels. Driving electric or hybrid cars also helps reduce air pollution. 
 Land pollution includes landfills overflowing with trash and any type of littering.	We can reduce land pollution by refusing to litter, recycling our trash, and volunteering to clean up our communities. Also, we can buy in bulk so that there is less packaging to throw away.

1. What are the two most important facts listed above? Explain why you think each of these facts is important. Use the back of the page if you need more room.

____

____

____

____

2. Which of the suggestions listed above do you think would be the easiest to get most people to do?

____

Why? ______________________________

____

Name: ____

Start a Movement!

You don't have to be an adult to change the world. Kids can make a big difference. You can create big change by starting a movement in your community. This was certainly the case for Chase and Vance, two Boy Scouts on a mission.

It all started when Chase and Vance saw a giant pile of books that were on the way to a landfill. The two boys decided to **reduce** waste and save the books. This is how their project, *read.repeat.*, was born.

The goal of *read.repeat.* is to collect used books and send them to places that need them. Chase and Vance have donated books to schools, hospitals, and libraries. By doing so, the two boys prevent unnecessary waste and provide a great service to their community.

In just a few years, Chase and Vance have collected more than 47,000 books. They have donated over 44,000 of these books. In the future, *read.repeat.* hopes to donate 50,000 books each year!

1. What does the word *reduce* likely mean?
   - **a.** to make larger
   - **b.** to refill often
   - **c.** to make smaller
   - **d.** to wash away

2. This passage is mainly about ____________________.
   - **a.** how to start your own environmental movement
   - **b.** how two boys made a big difference in their community
   - **c.** the importance of reading
   - **d.** the best way to recycle

3. What kind of movement could you create to help the environment?

____

____

____

____

____

Name: ______________________________

Word Study—Reducing Our Impact

Directions: Study the definitions. Then, use each vocabulary word in a sentence that relates to the information from this unit.

environment—the natural world

____

____

____

fossil fuel—a fuel (natural gas, coal, and/or oil) formed in the Earth from plant or animal remains

____

____

____

recycle—to send (used papers, bottles, cans, etc.) to a place where they are made into something new

____

____

____

reduce—to make smaller in size, amount, or number; to decrease

____

____

____

toxic—containing poisonous substances; poisonous

____

____

____

Name: ______________________________

Pollution I See

Directions: Complete the chart below. What types of pollution do you see in your daily life? How can you help?

Pollution I See	How I Can Help

Name: ______________________________

My Movement

Directions: Think about how you can help the environment. Answer the questions below. Then, plan your movement!

1. What type of pollution will your movement focus on: water, air, or land pollution?

   ____

2. How will you reduce pollution? Write a paragraph describing your plan.

   ____

   ____

   ____

   ____

   ____

3. What are the goals of your movement?

   ____

   ____

   ____

Directions: Design an e-flyer that you can post on social media.

____

(Name of Movement)

____

(Write a statement to describe your movement.)

____

____

____

____

(Draw an image that represents your movement.)

Movement Goals:

1. ______________________________

2. ______________________________

Tracking Sheet

Unit 1 *(pages 6–10)*	
Defining Energy	
Hold on Tight!	
Potential or Kinetic Energy?	
Energy Forms	
Word Study—Intro to Energy	
I See Energy	
Unit 2 *(pages 11–15)*	
Let There Be Light!	
Light Waves	
Word Study—The Power of Light	
Understanding Light Waves	
My Science Blog—Light Energy	
Unit 3 *(pages 16–22)*	
All About Sound	
Light and Sound	
Underwater Waves	
Dolphin Echolocation	
Word Study—The "How" of Sound	
A Dolphin Tale	
Unit 4 *(pages 23–27)*	
Changes in Energy	
Energy Conversions	
Word Study—Energy: Conversions and Collisions	
Crash! Boom! Pow!	
Energy at Work: Baseball	
Unit 5 *(pages 28–32)*	
Natural Wonder	
Waves Are Natural Wonders	
Deadly Waves	
Word Study—The Wonder of Waves	
Writing the Waves	
Unit 6 *(pages 33–37)*	
Eye Spy	
In the Eye	
Seeing in the Dark	
Word Study—Light and Sight	
Is Light Important?	

Unit 7 *(pages 38–42)*	
The Wonders of the Human Brain	
The Three Parts of the Brain	
A Day in the Great Outdoors	
Word Study—The Human Brain	
The Power of the Brain	
Unit 8 *(pages 43–47)*	
Fennec Foxes—Tiny but Tough	
Survival in the Desert	
The Sneaky Sidewinder	
Word Study—Surviving in the Wild	
Adapting to the Desert	
Unit 9 *(pages 48–51)*	
Groups in the Wild	
Understanding Animal Groups	
Word Study—Animal Groups	
Protecting the Young	
Writing About Animal Groups	
Unit 10 *(pages 52–56)*	
Growing Together	
Photosynthesis	
Anatomy of a Plant	
Word Study—What a Plant Needs to Grow	
The Structure of a Plant	
Unit 11 *(pages 57–61)*	
Let's Rock and Roll!	
Three Kinds of Rocks	
Reading the Rocks	
Word Study—Rock Types	
Rock Comics	
Unit 12 *(pages 62–66)*	
Forces of Nature	
Three Types of Weathering	
Carried Away	
Word Study—Weathering and Erosion	
Weathering vs. Erosion	
Unit 13 *(pages 67–70)*	
Blast from the Past	
A Fantastic Find	
Word Study—Fossils	
Featuring Fossils	

Unit 14 *(pages 71–74)*	
Journey Through Earth	
Earth's Layers	
Word Study—Layers of Earth	
My Great Journey	
Unit 15 *(pages 75–79)*	
Kaboom!	
Word Study—Volcanoes	
Parts of a Volcano	
Understanding Volcanoes	
On Krakatoa	
Unit 16 *(pages 80–83)*	
Terrible Temblors	
Word Study—Earthquakes	
Three Types of Plate Boundaries	
Writing About Earthquakes	
Unit 17 *(pages 84–89)*	
Ready for Anything	
Superior Structures	
Word Study—Preparing for Earthquakes	
The Taipei 101 Skyscraper	
Thinking Like an Engineer	
Unit 18 *(pages 90–95)*	
Flood Alert!	
Word Study—Floods	
A Safer Space	
Preparing for a Flood	
Flood Ready	
Unit 19 *(pages 96–100)*	
Earth's Resources	
Types of Resources	
The Fuel of Modern Life	
Word Study—Natural Resources	
My Science Blog—Natural Resources	
Unit 20 *(pages 101–106)*	
The Way We Live Matters	
Types of Pollution and How to Help	
Start a Movement!	
Word Study—Reducing Our Impact	
Pollution I See	
My Movement	

Answer Key

Unit 1—Intro to Energy

Defining Energy (page 6)

1. b
2. c
3. b
4. Check for appropriate answers.

Hold on Tight! (page 7)

1. b
2. c
3. Answers will vary but students should mention that potential energy is stored energy and kinetic energy is energy in motion.

Potential or Kinetic Energy? (page 8)

1. kinetic
2. kinetic
3. potential
4. kinetic
5. potential
6. potential
7. kinetic
8. potential
9. kinetic
10. potential

Draw It! Check student drawings for appropriate answers.

Energy Forms (page 9)

1. c
2. a
3. b

Word Study—Intro to Energy (page 9)

Check for appropriate answers.

I See Energy (page 10)

Check that students have written about potential and kinetic energy, including examples they see at school and on the playground.

Unit 2—The Power of Light

Let There Be Light! (page 11)

1. c
2. kinetic
3. b

Light Waves (page 12)

1. a
2. crest, trough
3. Possible answers:
   a. *waves shorter than visible light:* ultraviolet rays, X-rays, gamma rays
   b. *visible light waves:* colors of the rainbow
   c. *waves longer than visible light:* infrared rays (radiator or lighting a fire), microwaves (phone signals and microwave ovens), radio waves (radio and television broadcasts)

Word Study—The Power of Light (page 13)

Check for appropriate answers.

Understanding Light Waves (page 14)

1. kinetic
2. crest
3. infrared
4. visible
5. shorter
6. wavelength
7. Radio
8. waves
9. trough
10. longer
11. Microwaves
12. potential

My Science Blog—Light Energy (page 15)

Check that students have written about light energy, including details about light waves with short, medium, and long wavelengths.

Unit 3—The "How" of Sound

All About Sound (page 16)

1. vibrates
2. c
3. Check for appropriate answers.

Light and Sound (page 18)

Possible answers for Venn diagram:

Light

- Plants and animals need light to survive.
- The Sun is a source of light.
- Light and heat energy are found together.
- The colors we see are determined by the wavelength of light.

Sound

- Sound waves happen when an object vibrates.
- Sound can be loud or soft.
- Sound can be high or low pitch.
- The stronger an object vibrates, the louder the sound will be.

Both

- Light waves and sound waves send signals to our brain.
- Light and sound are both forms of kinetic energy.
- Light and sound both travel. Light travels at 186,282 miles per second. Sound can travel at 1,100 feet per second.

Underwater Waves (page 19)

1. 4, 1, 3, 2, 5
2. b
3. Check for appropriate answers.

Dolphin Echolocation (page 20)

Check that students have correctly described the process of dolphin echolocation.

Word Study—The "How" of Sound (page 21)

Check for appropriate answers.

A Dolphin Tale (page 22)

Check for appropriate answers.

Unit 4—Energy—Conversions and Collisions

Changes in Energy (page 23)

1. c
2. b
3. conversion
4. Check for appropriate answers.

Energy Conversions (page 24)

1. light, chemical
2. electrical, heat
3. conversion, sound

Answer Key *(cont.)*

Word Study—Energy: Conversions and Collisions (page 25)
Check for appropriate answers.

Crash! Boom! Pow! (page 26)

1. d
2. transfer
3. Check for appropriate answers.

Energy at Work: Baseball (page 27)

1. Answers will vary, but students may mention that there is a transfer of kinetic energy between the bat and ball. This transfer of energy causes the ball to move in a different direction. Energy is also transferred into the air, creating the crack sound of the bat hitting the ball.
2. Answers will vary, but students may mention that the player is converting chemical energy into kinetic energy while running across the field.
3. Answers will vary, but students may mention that electrical energy is converted into light energy when night-game lights are turned on.

Unit 5—The Wonder of Waves

Natural Wonder (page 28)

1. Details 1 and 3 should be circled.
2. c
3. Check for appropriate answers.

Waves Are Natural Wonders (page 29)

1. Wavelength is found by measuring the distance between two wave crests.
2. In any order: trough, crest.
3. Check for appropriate answers.
4. Check student drawings for appropriate answers.

Deadly Waves (page 30)

1. c
2. a
3. c
4. Check for appropriate answers.

Word Study—The Wonder of Waves (page 31)

1. c 2. e 3. a 4. f 5. d 6. b

Label It! Check for appropriate answers.

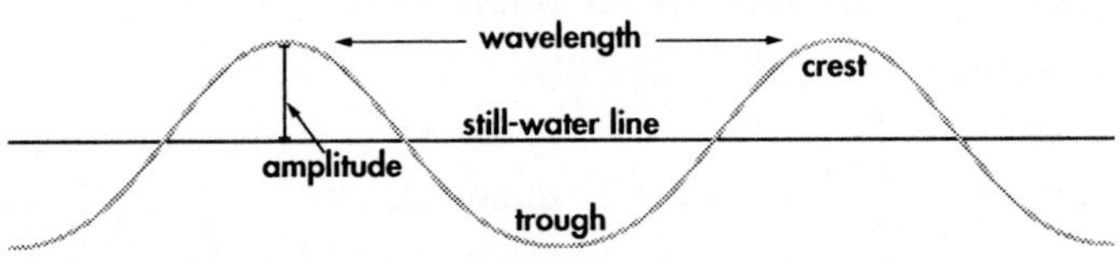

Writing the Waves (page 32)
Check that students have written articles describing the parts of a wave and included information related to tsunamis.

Unit 6—Light and Sight

Eye Spy (page 33)

1. c
2. Facts 1 and 3 should be checked.
3. 2, 1, 4, 5, 3, 7, 6

In the Eye (page 34)

1. retina
2. Light
3. lens
4. cornea
5. iris
6. pupil

Seeing in the Dark (page 35)

1. c
2. Causes 2 and 4 should be circled.
3. Check for appropriate answers.

Word Study—Light and Sight (page 36)
Check for appropriate answers.

Is Light Important? (page 37)
Check that students have written about the connection between light and sight.

Unit 7—The Human Brain

The Wonders of the Human Brain (page 38)

1. In any order: cerebrum, brain stem, and cerebellum
2. a
3. c
4. Check for appropriate answers.

The Three Parts of the Brain (page 39)
Check for appropriate answers.

A Day in the Great Outdoors (page 40)

1. c
2. b
3. d
4. Check for appropriate answers.

Word Study—The Human Brain (page 41)
Check for appropriate answers.

The Power of the Brain (page 42)
Check for appropriate answers.

Unit 8—Surviving in the Wild

Fennec Foxes: Tiny but Tough (page 43)

1. b
2. a
3. b
4. Check for appropriate answers.

Survival in the Desert (page 44)
Check that students have written three details that support the main idea.

The Sneaky Sidewinder (page 45)

1. c
2. a
3. b
4. Check for appropriate answers.

Answer Key *(cont.)*

Word Study—Surviving in the Wild (page 46)
Check for appropriate answers.

Adapting to the Desert (page 47)
Check for appropriate answers.

Unit 9—Animal Groups

Groups in the Wild (page 48)

1. hierarchy
2. b
3. Check for appropriate answers.

Understanding Animal Groups (page 49)

1. b 2. c 3. a

Word Study—Animal Groups (page 49)
Check for appropriate answers.

Protecting the Young (page 50)

1. d
2. predators
3. Check for appropriate answers.

Writing About Animal Groups (page 51)
Check that students have written about how animals behave in groups and how their behavior helps them survive.

Unit 10—What a Plant Needs to Grow

Growing Together (page 52)

1. Causes 2 and 4 should be circled.
2. b
3. Check for appropriate answers.

Photosynthesis (page 53)
Check that students have correctly described the process of photosynthesis.

Anatomy of a Plant (page 54)

1. b
2. Students should explain that a stable plant is one that stands firmly and does not fall over.
3. Check for appropriate answers.

Word Study—What a Plant Needs to Grow (page 55)
Check for appropriate answers.

The Structure of a Plant (page 56)
Check that students have written about how a plant's structure supports its growth and survival.

Unit 11—Rock Types

Let's Rock and Roll! (page 57)

1. b
2. igneous (b), sedimentary (a), metamorphic (c)
3. c
4. Check for appropriate answers.

Three Kinds of Rocks (page 58)
Check for appropriate answers.

Reading the Rocks (page 59)

1. c
2. d
3. Check for appropriate answers.

Word Study—Rock Types (page 60)
Check for appropriate answers.

Rock Comics (page 61)
Check that student comics include facts about rocks.

Unit 12—Weathering and Erosion

Forces of Nature (page 62)

1. a
2. Weathering
3. Check for appropriate answers.

Three Types of Weathering (page 63)

1. Answers will vary, but students may mention that biological weathering is caused by living things and physical weathering is caused by wind, water, and changes in temperature.
2. Answers will vary, but students may mention that all three types of weathering wear down rocks over time.
3. Check for appropriate answers.

Carried Away (page 64)

1. erosion
2. b
3. Check for appropriate answers.

Word Study—Weathering and Erosion (page 65)
Check for appropriate answers.

Weathering vs. Erosion (page 66)
Check for appropriate answers.

Unit 13—Fossils

Blast from the Past (page 67)

1. d
2. fossils
3. Check for appropriate answers.

A Fantastic Find (page 68)

1. b
2. d
3. Check for appropriate answers.

Word Study—Fossils (page 69)
Check for appropriate answers.

Featuring Fossils (page 70)
Check that students have written articles about fossils, including examples of fossils and describing how they are formed.

Answer Key *(cont.)*

Unit 14—Layers of Earth

Journey Through Earth (page 71)

1. crust, mantle, outer core, inner core
2. Check for appropriate answers.

Earth's Layers (page 72)

1. d   2. c   3. e   4. b   5. a

Label It! Check that students have correctly labeled the graphic.

1. the crust
2. inner core, outer core, mantle, crust

Word Study—Layers of Earth (page 73)

Check for appropriate answers.

My Great Journey (page 74)

Check that student comics include facts about the layers of Earth.

Unit 15—Volcanoes

Kaboom! (page 75)

1. dormant   2. c
3. Check for appropriate answers.

Word Study—Volcanoes (page 76)

Check for appropriate answers.

Parts of a Volcano (page 77)

1. In any order: lava, ash
2. a
3. Check for appropriate answers.

Understanding Volcanoes (page 78)

1. b   3. h   5. f   7. c
2. e   4. g   6. a   8. d

Label It! Check that students have correctly labeled the graphic. Use page 77 as a guide.

On Krakatoa (page 79)

Check for appropriate responses.

Unit 16—Earthquakes

Terrible Temblors (page 80)

1. Possible answers: plates, tectonic plates, or rock masses
2. fault
3. 2, 4, 1, 5, 3

Word Study—Earthquakes (page 81)

Check for appropriate answers

Three Types of Plate Boundaries (page 82)

1. transform   2. convergent   3. divergent

Writing About Earthquakes (page 83)

1. Answers will vary, but students may mention that tectonic plates are moving rock masses that make up Earth's crust.
2. Answers will vary, but students may mention that tectonic plates have different types of boundaries. Sometimes they move toward each other, as in a convergent plate boundary. Sometimes they move away from each other, as in a divergent plate boundary, and sometimes they slide alongside each other, as in a transform plate boundary.
3. Answers will vary, but students may mention that when tectonic plates move abruptly along a fault, seismic waves occur, creating an earthquake.

Unit 17—Preparing for Earthquakes

Ready for Anything (page 84)

1. secured
2. hazards
3. b
4. Check for appropriate answers.

Superior Structures (page 85)

1. b   2. d
3. Check for appropriate answers.

Word Study—Preparing for Earthquakes (page 86)

Check for appropriate answers.

The Taipei 101 Skyscraper (page 88)

Check for appropriate answers.

Thinking Like an Engineer (page 89)

Check that student responses and drawings are appropriate.

Unit 18—Floods

Flood Alert! (page 90)

1. c
2. Student answers may vary but students should list two examples of structures that prevent flooding such as dams and levees.
3. Check for appropriate answers.

Word Study—Floods (page 91)

Check for appropriate answers.

A Safer Space (pages 92–93)

1. b   2. elevate
3. Check for appropriate answers.

Answer Key *(cont.)*

Preparing for a Flood (page 94)

1. Dams
2. pump
3. prevent
4. Artificial
5. tsunamis
6. sealant
7. elevate
8. levee

Draw It! Check that student responses and drawings are appropriate.

Flood Ready (page 95)

Check for appropriate answers.

Unit 19—Natural Resources

Earth's Resources (page 96)

1. In any order: renewable, nonrenewable
2. nonrenewable; they take a long time to be created by nature
3. renewable; they are easily created by nature

Types of Resources (page 97)

1. renewable; answers will vary, but students may mention that plants grow quickly and are easy for nature to make
2. renewable; answers will vary, but students may mention that sunlight is always available
3. nonrenewable; answers will vary, but students may mention that oil takes a long time for nature to make
4. nonrenewable; answers will vary, but students may mention that coal takes a long time for nature to make

The Fuel of Modern Life (page 98)

1. b
2. Facts 2 and 3 should be checked.
3. Check for appropriate answers.

Word Study—Natural Resources (page 99)

Check for appropriate answers.

My Science Blog—Natural Resources (page 100)

Check that students have written about natural resources, including facts about fossil fuels and examples of renewable and nonrenewable resources.

Unit 20—Reducing Our Impact

The Way We Live Matters (page 101)

1. c
2. Details 2 and 4 should be circled.
3. Check for appropriate answers.

Types of Pollution and How to Help (page 102)

1. Check for appropriate answers.
2. Check for appropriate answers.

Start a Movement! (page 103)

1. c
2. b
3. Check for appropriate answers.

Word Study—Reducing Our Impact (page 104)

Check for appropriate answers.

Pollution I See (page 105)

Check for appropriate answers.

My Movement (page 106)

1. Possible answers: water, air, or land.
2. Check for appropriate answers.
3. Check for appropriate answers.

My E-flyer: Check that students have designed an e-flyer that includes an illustration and describes their environmental movement.